Stuck in the Semi-Periphery?

Richard Filcak

Stuck in the
Semi-Periphery?

Central Europe Between Capitalism
and Climate Change

PETER LANG

Berlin · Bruxelles · Chennai · Lausanne · New York · Oxford

Bibliographic Information published by the Deutsche Nationalbibliothek
The Deutsche Nationalbibliothek lists this publication in the Deutsche
Nationalbibliografie; detailed bibliographic data is available
online at http://dnb.d-nb.de.

Library of Congress Control Number: 2025040486

© Cover image: Richard Filcak

ISBN 978-3-631-93878-2 (Print)
ISBN 978-3-631-93865-2 (E-PDF)
ISBN 978-3-631-93879-9 (E-PUB)
DOI 10.3726/b22963

© 2026 Peter Lang Group AG, Lausanne (Switzerland)
Published by Peter Lang GmbH, Berlin (Germany)

info@peterlang.com

This publication has been peer reviewed.

www.peterlang.com

Table of Contents

TABLE OF CONTENTS

List of Figures

Foreword

There is perhaps no better illustration of the absurd system we live in than the Arctic region. While climate experts point to catastrophic events and the rapid acceleration of climate change due to melting ice, others see emerging business opportunities in shipping and potential access to rich deposits of oil, gas, and rare earth metals – driven by demand from the manufacturing of military equipment, electric cars, and wind turbines. The paradox of climate change is that as the planet heats up, more money can be made from these opportunities – but for how long? This book aims to help us understand how we reached this point and what alternatives exist from a Central European perspective. Central Europe's journey – from the struggles of industrialisation to the political shifts of the 1990s and its subsequent integration into the European Union – serves as a lens through which we can better comprehend both global and local climate change challenges.

The point of departure is that if we want to address adverse climate trends, we need to understand the world we have built. This book critically assesses the intersection of geopolitics, capitalism, and environmental policy, offering a nuanced discussion of the contradictions inherent in the current system. It explores key issues such as the tension between the systemic need for economic growth – often pursued regardless of ecological limits – the imbalance between public and private interests, and the geopolitical challenges of achieving climate neutrality. The role of the European Union's Green Deal and its impact on Central Europe are discussed in depth, particularly regarding competitiveness, security, and the socio-economic consequences of decarbonisation. A recurring question in this book – perhaps an idealistic one – is this: Is it possible, and at what cost, to shift away from a system based on competition, overproduction, and overconsumption toward one grounded in sustainability and capable of addressing climate change? Or is the more realistic scenario one of growing inequalities, insecurity, and a relentless march toward climate catastrophe?

List of Abbreviations

CBAM	Carbon Border Adjustment Mechanism
COMECON	The Council for Mutual Economic Assistance
ECB	European Central Bank
EC	European Commission
ECA	European Court of Auditors
EEA	European Environment Agency
EGD	European Green Deal
ETS	Emissions Trading System
EU	European Union
IPPC	Intergovernmental Panel on Climate Change
REACH	Registration, Evaluation, Authorisation and Restriction of Chemicals
TEEB	The Economics of Ecosystems and Biodiversity
UNDESA	Department of Economic and Social Affairs of the United Nations Secretariat
UNFCCC	United Nations Framework Convention on Climate Change
UNHCR	United Nations High Commissioner for Refugees
US	United Stated of America
WCED	World Commission on Environment and Development
WEF	World Economic Forum

List of Abbreviations

Introduction

The idea for this book has been developing for some time, but the definitive impetus came from watching the debate between John Mearsheimer and Jeffrey Sachs at the All-In Summit 2024. This clash of ideas between two leading global thinkers – Mearsheimer, who described the iron logic of geopolitics leading to competition and conflict, and Sachs, who advocated for a vision of a world built on cooperation and sustainability in the face of global challenges – highlighted the widening gap between where we need to go and where we are currently heading. While there has undoubtedly been significant progress in climate policy over recent decades – from the 1992 United Nations Framework Convention on Climate Change at the Rio Summit, to the Kyoto Protocol and the 2015 Paris Agreement – global greenhouse gas emissions continue to rise, pushing us closer to a catastrophic outcome.

The changing situation in the Arctic region illustrates the logic of the system we've built. While climate experts point to the catastrophic real-time events and the acceleration of climate change caused by melting ice, others see emerging business opportunities – in shipping, which rose by 37% over the decade leading up to 2024, or in the potential access to rich deposits of oil, gas, and rare earth metals. The demand for rare earth metals, essential for manufacturing military equipment, electric cars, and wind turbines, further exacerbates this paradox. Climate change, in this context, opens yet another space for geopolitical confrontation between the West and Russia, backed by China. The 2024 ridiculous demand of the newly elected American president to take over control of Greenland points to geopolitical threats we are facing in the future but may also reflect deeper structural problems of Western capitalism.

Early in the twentieth century, Joseph Schumpeter, one of the most influential political economists, popularised the term 'creative destruction'. It describes a process of industrial mutation that continually overturns the economic structure from within – destroying the old while continually creating the new (Schumpeter 2021). The 'old' must give way to the 'new', which will better adapt to the needs of capital and offer new opportunities for prosperity.

A century later, humanity faces perhaps the biggest existential threat in history: climate change. The policy response to the ongoing and anticipated impacts of global warming lies in the creative replacement of the old fossil fuel-powered system with a new, decarbonised, and climate-neutral economy. The emerging but fragile global framework of climate change treaties and goals took a serious blow when the US made the unilateral decision to withdraw from the Paris Agreement in 2025. We will only know in retrospect whether this was a temporary bump in the road or the start of global escalations, where climate change becomes one of the first victims.

The European Union, at least in rhetoric, is currently a strong advocate for climate action, recently reaffirming its commitment to climate neutrality by 2050. In practice, this means reducing greenhouse gas emissions to an absolute minimum, with any remaining emissions to be compensated through natural and artificial carbon sequestration. Yet, factors such as the dynamics of the economic system, overarching geopolitical realities, and internal tensions hinder effective action. For countries or regions that want to stay on the path of climate agreements, the global context presents an analogy to the prisoner's dilemma, where rational agents may either cooperate for mutual benefit or betray their partner for individual gain. Defecting is rational, but cooperation yields a higher payoff for all ...

The transformation of the European economy through decarbonisation can be understood as a dilemma: how fast to move in the uncertain global context? From Schumpeter's perspective, it is a challenge to manage a process of creative destruction and industrial mutation on a scale comparable only to the era of massive electrification in the late nineteenth century. Yet electrification correlated from the start with technological progress, high productivity, and economic growth. Driven by vested interests of capital, if nothing else, workers' productivity skyrocketed. Vladimir Lenin, the fresh winner of the proletariat revolution in Russia, noted on the central importance of electrification: 'Communism is Soviet power plus the electrification of the whole country.'

Decarbonisation, for many in the political discourse, represents the opposite – creative destruction leading to decline. An obsolete investment that decreases productivity, increases energy prices, and slows down growth. The problem begins with the very basic understanding of the need to address climate change. There are those who firmly understand the need to, if not stop, at least slow down climate change, and then there are those who either do not believe it is a substantial problem or who cynically prefer short-term gains over long-term issues. Counter-narratives operate with the goal of revolutionising the economic structure into a climate-resilient system that will foster development, create new employment opportunities, and new forms of well-being – all without addressing the roots of the system.

This book is written from the perspective of the real and present threat of climate change, as we will refer to data and facts based on the best available global science. However, this position is also based on the need to analyse capitalism as the dominant global economic system. We need to understand why the climate neutrality of the global economic system faces multiple challenges as soon as it confronts the logic of geopolitics and neoliberal state progress.

Analyses and outlooks for the transition to a climate-neutral economy in Europe, and specifically in Central Europe, highlight the unprecedented complexity of the transformation, the resistance of the system, and the limits imposed by the system's inherent logic. In other words, how far can we get through ecological modernisation, greening of capitalism, and a belief in changes in human behaviour? We need much more than to live in the illusion that significant change can occur if we all better understand the problems, get involved, and change our individual consumption.

For the 'enlightened' political elites, talking about decarbonisation policies presents a situation between a rock and a hard place. Even those who understand the scale of the climate catastrophes we face find it difficult to open crucial questions about the future of our system – questions which have been the same since the beginning of the Industrial Revolution. These questions deal with the legitimacy of the system, whether the market is a means or an end, and who benefits from the races.

The transformation of the European economy, transitioning from over 250 years of industrialisation based on coal, iron, and later oil, has been driven by pressures from climate change. But for Europe – and Central Europe specifically – it is also an attempt to address new competitiveness and security challenges. The new structures, emerging from the ruins of old industries and supported by European Union and member state policy frameworks, find themselves exposed to fierce global competition. EU and state interventions are deployed as temporary measures to enable the evolution of a new economic system based on clean industry and a green economy, but they can hardly address the structural conditions within the system.

Mainstream debates attempt to convince us that we are all in the same boat – whether as shareholders, factory owners, or assembly line workers. While it is true that we share a dependence on modern infrastructure, the reality from a climate perspective is different. The assembly line worker, much like a stoker on the Titanic, has little influence over the ship's course and enjoys only limited benefits from the wealth generated by the company owning the boat. Ultimately, their chances of protecting themselves from the adverse effects of climate change are far lower than those of the first-class passengers.

The dark side of large-scale industrial transformations primarily lies in the redistribution of economic benefits and social costs, or who will get what. Closures or the mining of heavy industry have been accompanied by long periods of stagnation and marginalisation in many regions, with different countries having varying degrees of success in addressing the negative effects. The United Kingdom's mine closures in the 1980s serve as a prime example of how the absence of policies within a neoliberal framework can lead to decline and long-term adverse impacts on people. It is not surprising that many in Central Europe who experienced the economic misery of the rapid neoliberal transformation in the 1990s are now prone to narratives of the status quo – the devil we know – rather than an uncertain future with unpredictable social consequences of policies as seen in the past deindustrialisation of the region.

The EU faces substantial pressure from member states, especially in Central Europe, to maintain the current production model – prioritising security, reducing migration, and increasing military expenditures. Global geopolitics are redefining the EU's role in a polarised world, calling for strategies to keep pace in technological advancements with global superpowers like the United States and China. Global instability, driven by competition, calls for protective measures and armament, which is an expensive business. So too are real solutions to climate change – there are investments that lead to destruction and those that prevent it.

Solutions are like the tip of an iceberg – the visible part is only a small fraction of the larger body of evidence, analysis, and interpretation beneath the surface. With this understanding, the search for alternatives must focus on building a foundation of knowledge and fostering discussions. The question of time remains critical: do we have enough of it to identify and implement solutions, or will we, like passengers on a sinking ship, end up arguing over who is to blame, how to pump the water out, and whether there's even a hole at all?

About the Book

This book aims to examine climate change as a problem deeply rooted in the economic and social context of our societies, exploring the limits and alternatives of the system from the perspective of Central Europe, a region located on the semi-periphery of core economic countries.

To address contemporary challenges, we must first understand history and how we arrived at this juncture. Modern society, as we know it, has its roots in the Industrial Revolution and was built on the paradigm of capital growth. In the opening section of this book, we revisit history with a particular focus on Central Europe. Since the mid-eighteenth century, the expansion of industrial production and agriculture enabled advancements in science, economics, and education. Economic progress allowed many people to climb the social ladder and freed large portions of the population from gruelling labour for starvation wages. However, the social and environmental consequences of this progress have remained a persistent thread throughout history, raising critical questions about our future direction in the age of climate change.

The emergence of industrial society began to transform Central Europe as early as the 1870s. It brought a greater pluralism of opinions and demands, influencing politics and economics. Over time, business, intertwined with politics, became the dominant force. After World War II, Central Europe experienced four decades of attempts to construct an alternative to capitalism – an alternative built on ideas of mass production and self-sufficiency, later accompanied by the drive to keep pace with mass production and consumer society emerging behind the Iron Curtain in the West.

The rapid transformation from centrally planned economies to market-driven economies began in the 1990s. In its early phases, this transition led to widespread deindustrialisation, impoverishment, and a declining quality of life. In the absence of any stronger domestic visions, the European Union was seen as a project offering hope, stability, vision, and new opportunities. Poland, the Czech Republic, Hungary, and Slovakia joined the EU in 2004. After more than two decades of membership, the very same Union is increasingly targeted for criticism in the region. The most visible part of this criticism is the European Green Deal and its climate and environmental policies, which are often seen by critics as detached from reality and detrimental to economic prosperity.

In retrospect, the environment has always been at the crossroads of competing interests – a dynamic that persists today. These competing interests lead to inevitable conflicts, which this book examines as tensions and conflicts between the ideal of a self-regulating market and the ecological limits to growth; public and private interests; solutions within the current system versus those requiring systemic or alternative systemic change; ideological premises and real-world applications; and the profitability and competitiveness of businesses versus the economic costs of environmental protection. Finally, it is crucial to understand the conflict between those who accumulate profits and those disproportionately exposed to environmental and climate risks, whether locally or globally.

The opening section of the book focuses on a brief history of Europe, and specifically Central Europe, illustrating how it evolved from a divided continent to one economic block unified under capitalism as the dominant system. This historical context shapes our present ideas and positions on climate change and the creative destruction necessary to transition towards climate neutrality.

The second section focuses on why climate change poses a critical challenge for Europe, the emerging framework of policies and responses, and their weaknesses. While progress is evident, the European Union lags in the global competition for technological dominance. Central European countries, with their weaker technological infrastructure, dependence on foreign investment, and challenges in demographics and fiscal stability, lack the resources necessary for substantial climate investments.

This section delves into the EU's emerging framework of competitiveness, security, and fairness, underpinned by its pursuit of strategic autonomy.

Despite criticism from political factions and member states, the EU's policy direction remains largely consistent. The European Green Deal represents not only a critical response to the environmental crisis but also a transformative economic and technological shift. This section critically examines the EU's ambitious goal of climate neutrality by 2050 and its implications for Central Europe.

The third section examines Europe's climate dilemmas at the intersection of geopolitics, capitalism, and social implications. It reflects on the possibility of a global economic and social shift, exploring the gap between the world as it is and the world as it should be. Can Europe create a model that balances competitiveness, security, and fairness? The global clash between geopolitics and the urgent need for radical decarbonisation shapes today's policies. This chapter situates the current situation within the economic foundation of our global system – capitalism – and questions whether environmental modernisation can reform it. Can capitalism be greened while maintaining an international order rooted in competition among established and emerging superpowers?

While Europeans can be proud of many achievements, such as social progress, access to education, healthcare, and opportunities for self-fulfilment, these did not come easily. They were the outcomes of complex and often bloody conflicts. Despite detours into the blind alleys of totalitarian ideologies, Europe has (so far) always returned to universal values and human rights. Our present achievements are thanks to those who came before us. However, in the social sciences, alongside describing the current state, the key task is to identify and understand trends.

One significant trend shaping responses to climate change is the growing imbalance between public and private interests. We are witnessing unprecedented privatisation and commodification of natural resources and public goods. Free capital pushes for the privatisation of forests and land while driving speculative investments in commodities. Today's economic cycles confirm Marx's thesis about the concentration of wealth in fewer hands, amplifying social and environmental costs.

How these dynamics will evolve – whether they will spark counter-movements or further entrench inequalities – remains uncertain. Should we remain optimistic, or should we fear greater polarisation and the rise of new totalitarian regimes in the context of irreversible climate change? What does the future hold for Europe's socio-economic model and its ability to ensure a just transition?

The treadmill of production demands continuous growth, yet combating climate change requires significant reductions in material and energy use. Ecological modernisation has made progress in reducing environmental impacts in areas such as manufacturing, product use, and recycling. Regional decarbonisation and urban greening policies are also in place. However, in a global system predicated on capital accumulation and economic growth, these efforts are offset by the expanding scale of production and consumption. The vague, fast-moving target is achieving a global balance anchored in climate neutrality.

The final section revisits key political and socio-economic challenges to achieving a climate-neutral Europe. Can we avoid a Malthusian future where resource scarcity intersects with population growth in the Global South, prompting fortification in the North? Will social inequalities deepen, creating insurmountable barriers? Is it possible to strike a compromise between capital and the climate while ensuring social protection and eco-state?

European countries face growing threats and constraints. Will they adapt and resolve these contradictions within their current framework, or are we on the brink of nonlinear, tectonic shifts? As John Gray (2009) warned, the twenty-first century may be marked by wars, massacres, and forced migrations that make past tragedies seem like precursors. While we hope for better outcomes, we fear that things may need to get worse before they improve.

Central European Perspective

Amid conflicting opinions, data and trends reveal that the global economy is increasingly responding to demands for adaptation and shifting toward a low-carbon future. While this transition may not be occurring as quickly or as substantially as needed, the move towards renewable energy and green technologies is becoming essential for both national and corporate competitiveness.

Among European regions, one stands out as particularly vulnerable to the transformations associated with climate change: Central Europe. Although there is no universally agreed-upon definition of Central Europe's boundaries, it typically includes countries with shared historical ties, cultural similarities, and geographical proximity. In this book, I focus on the transformation of the Visegrád countries – Czech Republic, Poland, Hungary, and Slovakia – nations with distinct yet interconnected histories and shared socio-economic experiences of post-socialist transformation (Figure 1).

This region, situated in the heart of the European continent, is characterised by its historical, cultural, and geographical diversity, as well as its shared experiences and parallel trends in uneven development. Central Europe has long occupied the economic semi-periphery of the continent's core countries. It was a latecomer to the Industrial Revolution, a battlefield in two world wars, and a testing ground for central planning during the twentieth century. The 1990s brought a wave of massive privatisation, while the 2000s saw the region emerge as a European manufacturing hub.

The region is situated at the crossroads of different climate zones, making it susceptible to extreme weather events, such as heatwaves, flooding, and severe storms, as well as shifts in rainfall patterns. It is expected to experience rising temperatures, droughts, and unpredictable weather events, which could have major implications for agriculture, water resources, and infrastructure.

The particularly fragmented agricultural sectors in Hungary and Poland are sensitive to the risks of crop yield loss due to changes in precipitation patterns, droughts, and temperature extremes. At the same time, the region relies heavily on energy-intensive industries, such as coal mining, heavy manufacturing, and chemicals – all of which are vulnerable to outsourcing through carbon leakage and require significant investments. The transition to renewable energy sources like wind and solar is hindered by existing infrastructure and resistance from vested interests in the coal, nuclear, and oil industries.

Figure 1: Map of European countries referred to here as Central Europe.
Source: Created with mapchart.net (This work is licensed under a Creative Commons Attribution-ShareAlike 4.0 International Licence [CC BY-SA 4.0])

Central Europe can be understood through the lens of Immanuel Wallerstein's World-Systems Theory as a semi-periphery (Wallerstein 2000, 2004), exhibiting characteristics of both the core and the periphery. As Klein et al. (2017) argue, East Central Europe began to industrialise earlier than most of the global periphery and is therefore more accurately described as a 'half-periphery'. However, it has remained in this position, failing to catch up with, or even significantly narrow the gap vis-à-vis the European core of advanced economies.

Core regions are economically developed, industrialised, and dominant in global trade. They possess strong states, advanced technologies, and capital-intensive production, extracting resources and labour from the periphery and semi-periphery while producing high-value goods for export. They also control global financial and political institutions, shaping rules to their advantage. Semi-periphery regions, while more industrialised and developed than the periphery, remain economically and politically subordinate to the core. Acting as a buffer, the semi-periphery mitigates tensions between the core and periphery, exploiting the latter while being exploited by the former.

This dual position has historically shaped narratives of transformation, ranging from those about catching up with the core, to more critical perspectives on exploitation and inequalities. An important factor in this narrative is the shared memory and common experience of recent, often painful transformations. Historically, Central Europe was the heart of centrally planned manufacturing, home to industries such as steel production, textiles, and heavy machinery. During the latter half of the twentieth century, these industries fuelled the economy, provided well-paying jobs, and supported thriving communities.

The 1990s brought a radical transformation from centrally planned economies to market economies. Guided by neoliberal theories, these reforms introduced market-driven policies and restructured governance. This transformation included embedding financial orthodoxy, implementing pro-competitive industrial policies, reforming constitutional frameworks, and 'flexibilising' state apparatuses, leading to the creation of a contractual post-social state (Cerny and Evans 2001).

The transition was harsh. High unemployment, the closure of entire production chains, mass layoffs, and large-scale emigration became a reality. Despite efforts to revitalise these economies, many regions still struggle.

Economic inequality remains pronounced, and recovery has been uneven. Mass migration to core countries, interlinked with adverse demographic trends, undermines prospects. Meanwhile, automation poses a persistent threat, even in areas that have successfully attracted new industries. These challenges highlight the complexities of economic transitions and the lasting impacts of deindustrialisation on communities.

In the 2000s, negative trends were partially reversed through foreign direct investment, the relocation of manufacturing industries from Western to Eastern Europe, and the opening of European markets. Yet, to a great extent, it is the shared memory of industrial and economic decline that shapes public attitudes toward decarbonisation today. While Central Europe initially embraced the European Union as a safeguard against future challenges, this belief has increasingly been shaken. In national public debates, the EU is often portrayed as a weak and misguided entity, pursuing a path of decline – 'committing suicide in live broadcast'. What is frequently missing from these debates is a deeper understanding of climate change, the limitations of capitalism, and the scope of EU power within a shifting geopolitical framework.

The climate is changing, and so is Central Europe. The optimism of the 1990s is giving way to a more sobering realisation that the future is both complex and uncertain. Instead of textbook democracy, we see battles for resources and dominance. Discussions of liberalism are being replaced by analyses of the threats posed by proponents of illiberal democracy. Citizens' influence on public affairs is diminishing, while the power of large corporations, financial groups, and their sponsored political parties continues to grow. We are witnessing the gradual neoliberalisation and privatisation of the state.

Yet, Central Europe's unique experiences may also offer valuable perspectives. As the old core countries of the European West themselves become semi-peripheral in the new global order, we need to discuss the future of Europe. How can we preserve the environmental and social gains of past struggles, without succumbing to the allure of illiberal democracies or totalitarian states?

From Industrial Revolution to Greening Capitalism

The birth of modern industry originated in the United Kingdom and soon spread to the European continent, including Central European countries (Figure 2). Although there was a gap of nearly three decades between the industrial boom in Manchester and similar developments in what is today Katowice in Poland, Rožňava in Slovakia, and Miskolc in Hungary, the speed of industrial expansion remained remarkable. Within just ten years, industrialisation crossed the English Channel, and in less than thirty years, new factories had been established in Central Europe.

The Vítkovice Ironworks was founded in 1828 in what is now the Czech Republic, but it was only after the 1870s that modern know-how and machinery were brought in from the United Kingdom and Belgium. This was no coincidence. Central Europe had a crucial advantage – abundant deposits of coal and iron, two essential resources for industrialisation.

The Industrial Revolution transformed society on a massive scale, producing profound and complex social changes. Mass migration to cities began during this period, a trend that, to some extent, continues to this day. The environmental consequences were immediate and severe. Early industrial cities were characterised by smoke, filth, and poor living conditions. Basic services – such as access to clean drinking water, waste management, and the maintenance of streets and parks – were either inadequate or entirely absent. Urban infrastructure struggled to keep pace with the rapid expansion of industrialisation.

As a result, starting primarily after 1830 in the West and after 1870 in Central Europe, epidemics of cholera and typhus became common. These outbreaks were exacerbated by two of the major killers of the nineteenth century: air and water pollution, which led to widespread respiratory and digestive diseases (Hobsbawm, 1999: 64). Period paintings of Ostrava, Czech Republic, and illustrations of steelworks in Chorzów, Poland, near Katowice, depict the massive scale of pollution caused by hundreds of factories and chimneys. Interestingly, a substantial portion of air pollution stemmed from one of the key drivers of the Industrial Revolution – the coal-powered steam engine. This marked the beginning of human-induced climate change.

The economic and social effects of industrialisation became increasingly evident, sparking the first waves of criticism. Friedrich Engels, in his seminal work *The Condition of the Working Class in England* (1969: 43), provides a grim description of industrial areas around Manchester: *'The workmen's cottages are old, dirty, and the smallest that exist; the pavements are bumpy, one falls into ruts. Without sewers or proper pavements, heaps of waste and refuse, together with disease-producing filth, lie among the pools in every direction. The air is poisoned with the fumes of it all and heavy with the smoke of a dozen factory chimneys.'*

This was not merely the perspective of a left-wing intellectual. Michael Sadler, chairman of the English Parliamentary Committee on Industrial Enterprise, also documented the devastating conditions endured by industrial workers. In his 1832 report, he described witnessing long lines of men, women, boys, and girls: *'Stunted, sick, deformed, and ruined, they cross the stage, each with their own story of hardship – a living picture of man's cruelty to man'* (Sadler Committee Report, 1832).

New industrial hubs, such as Ostrava in the Czech Republic and Łódź in Poland, followed the same patterns of exploitation first observed in England. Unsurprisingly, these industrial centres became hotbeds of resistance, as labour movements grew increasingly organised in response to harsh working and living conditions.

In a system indifferent to social problems, it is hardly surprising that sensitivity to environmental issues would also be lacking. Swedish scientist Svante Arrhenius first identified in 1896 that changes in atmospheric carbon dioxide levels – caused by the Industrial Revolution – could

Figure 2: Spread of the Industrial Revolution in Europe.
Source: Based on data from Encyclopaedia Britannica.
Created with mapchart.net (This work is licensed under a Creative Commons Attribution-ShareAlike 4.0 International Licence [CC BY-SA 4.0])

significantly alter the Earth's surface temperature. Yet, it took nearly a century for climate change to be seriously acknowledged and placed on the policy agenda.

The conditions of workers gradually improved, primarily due to their growing organisation in trade unions and political parties. Some argue that, in a situation where a proletarian revolution always seemed imminent, capital had no choice but to grant certain rights and concessions. While the most appalling working conditions were eventually alleviated, deeper and more complex questions – such as the meaning and position of individuals in an industrialised society – remain relevant to this day. A powerful example of this is the theme of alienation in the era of industrial development, as depicted in Charlie Chaplin's film *Modern Times*.

It became increasingly evident that environmental degradation was not only an ecological issue but also one of inequality. While the affluent West End of London accumulated wealth, East London – due to prevailing winds – became a hotspot for air pollution. These emerging social and environmental conflicts found powerful expression in art and literature. Upton Sinclair's

The Jungle, published in 1906, dramatically exposed the harsh realities faced by workers in the meatpacking industry. The novel highlighted the dire consequences of an absence of social progress, combined with harsh living conditions in a polluted environment, where corruption and the rule of the powerful thrived.

The industrial practices and capital generated by the Industrial Revolution soon extended to other areas of human activity, including agriculture. John Steinbeck's The Grapes of Wrath portrays a story set against the backdrop of the 'Dust Bowl' phenomenon in America. Between 1930 and 1936 (in some places until 1940), a large-scale ecological disaster devastated the American and Canadian prairies. The displacement of small farmers, the rise of large industrialised farms, the introduction of heavy machinery, and unsustainable agricultural techniques – including deep ploughing and the absence of crop rotation – destroyed the natural grasses that once held the soil in place and retained moisture. When drought struck in the 1930s, the soil was left vulnerable to erosion, rising into massive dust storms that swept across the land. Winds carried the dust south and east, forcing thousands of bankrupt farm families to migrate to cities and other parts of the country. Once fertile lands were reduced to barren wastelands, marking one of the earliest recorded instances of large-scale environmental degradation and human displacement caused by industrial activity.

The same pattern of industrial pollution with severe consequences, now visible in parts of Asia and Africa, was once prevalent across Europe. The coal mining and metallurgical boom in the Ostrava region – now part of the Czech Republic – devastated the local environment. Particularly during the eighteenth and nineteenth centuries, this region was deeply intertwined with the rise of capitalism, the decline of feudalism, shifts in property ownership, and the expansion of large industrial enterprises within the Austro-Hungarian Monarchy (Martinec and Schejbalová, 2004).

The twentieth century witnessed a major social transformation in Central Europe. Industrial growth was widely regarded as a sign of modernisation, with factory chimneys symbolising progress. However, it also became increasingly clear that the interests of the general population did not always align with those of the economic elites who controlled and profited from industry.

1.1. From Malthus to Techno-Optimism: The Evolution of Environmental Thought

A look at history reveals that debates over regulation versus business interests, the social costs of development, and the balance between competitiveness and environmental measures are not recent concerns. Conflicts between nature conservation and economic and social priorities have existed for a long time.

The origins of modern environmental awareness, thought, and policies relevant to today's climate change challenges can be traced back to the second half of the twentieth century, particularly in Europe and the United States. It was in these regions that the key ideological and social movements influencing environmental policy and its practical application first emerged.

If we examine today's decarbonisation and climate neutrality agenda through a historical lens, we see both its foundations and the contradictions that have been present from the beginning. The roots of the current production and consumption system, which shape European approaches to climate change, lie in the mass production of goods and services – a feat that was not technically feasible before industrialisation. European history has undergone turbulent periods, including the division into two ideological blocs and subsequent unification after the 1990s. Yet, it remains inextricably tied to capitalism as the dominant economic system. Paradoxically, even the centrally planned socialist economies of the Eastern Bloc mimicked the West's production and consumption patterns. It took over a century from the beginning of the Industrial Revolution for both the West and the East to begin questioning the environmental limits of this system.

The idea of Earth as a bounded system that imposes restrictions on human activity is based on fundamental scientific facts. Aside from incoming solar energy (and minor cosmic dust), Earth functions as a closed system with finite renewable and non-renewable resources. Barry Commoner, in 1971, described the four laws of ecology: 1) everything is connected to everything else, 2) everything must go somewhere (nothing is lost in nature), 3) nature knows best and cannot be replaced by technology, and 4) nothing is free, and everything comes from somewhere.

However, the planet's resources seemed for a long time almost limitless in comparison to human needs. The eighteenth, nineteenth, and much of the twentieth century were marked by positivism and optimism in the social sciences, based on the assumption of continuous growth in an apparently boundless world. The question of the limits of economic development and planetary resources entered the discussion as a relevant problem only lately. This was not as obvious as it may seem from today's perspective.

The eighteenth century was the time of Thomas Malthus, an English scholar preoccupied with political economy and demography. Between 1798 and 1826, he published six editions of *An Essay on the Principle of Population*. In contrast to the prevailing belief in inevitable progress, Malthus argued that it was only a matter of time before society would be unable to produce enough food for its growing population, leading to famine, misery, and collapse.

His central assumption was that while population growth is geometric, agricultural output grows arithmetically. He predicted that, inevitably, agricultural production would fail to keep up with population growth. His work became one of the cornerstones of early debates on the limits of economic and demographic expansion.

As we know today, Malthus's dire predictions did not materialise, largely because he failed to account for advances in agricultural productivity. The development of new agricultural techniques and industrial innovations multiplied food production in ways he could not foresee. However, his fundamental insight – that the interplay between population growth, resource consumption, and human needs is central to humanity's ability to survive within environmental limits – remains relevant.

Malthus disrupted the prevailing optimism of the Enlightenment, which saw humanity as destined to conquer nature through reason and science (Barbosa, 2009: 27). His ideas were significant because they challenged the assumption of human dominion over nature and the belief in unlimited economic expansion. However, he overlooked environmental degradation, which, in his time, was not yet recognised as a major issue. Nonetheless, his theories inspired later discussions on the limits of growth. His warnings about the consequences of uncontrolled population growth sparked a debate that continues today.

Not only did scientific discourse evolve, but public perception also shifted. The once-dominant optimism about progress and technological advancement began to wane, as reflected in literature and art. Lord Byron's 1816 poem *Darkness* imagines a world where the sun has gone out, while H. G. Wells's 1895 novel *The Time Machine* set the stage for the dystopian and catastrophic literary genre.

The growing ability of agriculture and industry to sustain expanding populations initially undermined the pessimistic predictions of Malthus. His ideas were frequently cited as examples of misinterpretation and flawed forecasting. The era of technological and technocratic solutions took hold, reinforcing optimism in 'natural' progress and development.

However, as industrial growth and consumption intensified, the finite nature of natural resources and the limited capacity of ecosystems to absorb waste became increasingly evident. By the mid-twentieth century, concerns about resource depletion and environmental degradation entered the public discourse. Malthusian ideas about the dangers of unchecked growth gained new relevance – not just in isolated economic sectors like agriculture, but in the broader context of systemic environmental sustainability.

In 1972, at the request of the Club of Rome, a team led by Donella H. Meadows, along with Dennis L. Meadows, Jørgen Randers, and William W. Behrens, produced a report that was later published as *Limits to Growth* (Meadows et al., 1972). The report was based on computer simulations that analysed the long-term impacts of human activity on the planet. Enabled by advances in cybernetics, the study built upon the work of system theorists like Jay Forrester.

The authors modelled various scenarios based on five key variables: world population, industrialisation, pollution, natural resource use, and food production. Notably, climate change was not explicitly included as a factor, though the report did highlight environmental degradation and resource depletion – both of which are closely linked to modern climate challenges.

The study did not predict specific dates for collapse but instead analysed long-term trends and their potential consequences. Its key conclusion was that if growth continued unchecked, the collapse of ecosystems – and the human societies dependent on them – could occur within the twenty-first century. However, the authors also argued that this collapse could be prevented through early action, new policies, and technological innovation.

The publication of *Limits to Growth* sparked a significant backlash. The report and its authors faced sharp criticism, much like today's climate change researchers. Opponents falsely claimed that the book had predicted a global collapse by the end of the twentieth century, dismissing its findings as alarmist and inaccurate.

However, in 2008, Graham Turner reassessed the report's predictions, comparing the original 1972 projections with real-world data from 1970 to 2000. Using the same five variables and examining the original three scenarios developed by Meadows and her team, he found that the data closely matched the 'standard run' scenario – the baseline scenario assuming no major changes in policy or behaviour (Turner, 2008). His findings confirmed that the trends outlined in 1972 had largely played out as expected, reinforcing concerns about unsustainable development.

Turner's research is not an isolated effort. Since the 1970s, increasingly sophisticated studies have examined the environmental consequences of human activity. Three key publications in this field – the UN Environment Programme's *Global Environmental Outlooks*, the *Millennium Ecosystem Assessment*, and the reports of the *Intergovernmental Panel on Climate Change (IPCC)* – all confirm the fundamental trends outlined in *Limits to Growth*. The primary differences lie in the details: an acceleration of certain environmental changes, a deeper understanding of their causes and effects, and more precise data.

Thomas Malthus's work laid the foundation for modern debates about the sustainability of human-created economic and social systems. His ideas have influenced green political thought while also attracting criticism from those who view his reasoning as outdated. Opponents often cite *Limits to Growth* and its subsequent updates as examples of misguided Malthusian thinking, arguing that resource scarcity is not a real threat and that technological innovation will resolve climate challenges, just as it did in agriculture.

Today, the environmental debate has shifted from concerns about industrial production to a broader ideological divide. While techno-optimists advocate for solutions such as ecological modernisation and green growth within the framework of capitalism, the fundamental question remains: Can environmental and climate challenges truly be solved within a system driven by endless growth? The 'elephant in the room' remains the capitalist model itself.

1.2. Post-WWII World and Central Role of Oil

When considering the new wave of creative destruction and the transition to decarbonisation, we must recognise that economic progress in many parts of the world, including Central Europe, has been historically built on coal and later oil. This is particularly significant on both sides of the Iron Curtain in post-World War II Europe. While the post-war period is often referred to as the golden age of capitalism (Hobsbawm, 1994), it was equally the golden age of state-planned socialism.

Following the economic downturn caused by the Great Depression and the devastation of two world wars, the second half of the twentieth century ushered in an era of economic expansion and extensive social transformation. This period was marked by rapid technological advancements and significant progress in the social sciences. Post-war recovery, driven by Keynesian economic policies that stimulated both production and consumption, laid the foundation for prolonged economic growth that lasted until the 1970s. This boom was largely fuelled by a newly established global economic order and the widespread availability of relatively cheap oil – a key factor in today's greenhouse gas emissions crisis.

Perhaps the most crucial factor in this post-war development was the low price of oil, which emerged as the dominant energy source for both industry and households. Unlike coal, oil enabled the rapid expansion of mass transportation and individual mobility, fundamentally reshaping modern life. Its affordability and abundance catalysed industrial growth and transformed daily existence. However, oil prices have always been intertwined with international politics. From the end of World War II until the 1973 oil crisis, prices remained relatively stable and low – until oil-exporting countries broke the West's dominance over pricing for the first time.

By the time the era of cheap oil came to an end, the entire infrastructure and lifestyle of developed and developing nations had become deeply reliant on its consumption. Both Western and Eastern Europe were no exception, as their economies became structurally dependent on fossil fuels. Although Central Europe differed in many ways from the core Western economies, its reliance on fossil fuels – particularly oil – remains a shared characteristic. The challenge today lies in overcoming this deep-seated dependency and finding sustainable alternatives.

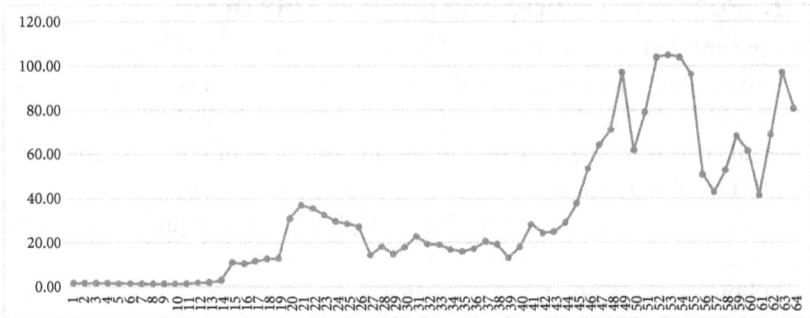

Figure 3: US crude oil first purchase price (in dollars per barrel) from 1974 to 2023. *Source:* Adapted from US data. Energy Information Administration[1].

In June 1944, representatives from forty-four countries met in Bretton Woods to discuss the creation of a new international economic system. The result was the Bretton Woods Agreement, which laid the foundation for the establishment of the International Monetary Fund (IMF) and committed nations to adopting monetary policies tied to the value of gold. Countries also agreed to reduce barriers to free trade and promote the development of a global market. While the system underwent significant changes after the US dollar abandoned the gold standard in 1971, it endured and fostered an environment conducive to international trade and gradual globalisation. This system enabled strong economic growth but also contributed to the globalised patterns of production and consumption seen today, along with the associated inequalities and environmental impacts. Moreover, it played a critical role in underpinning international trade in oil and the widespread reliance on fossil fuels.

Central Europe, as part of the Eastern Bloc, had access to oil from the Soviet Union, sourced from what are now Russia, Kazakhstan, and Azerbaijan. The price of oil was centrally planned and often included in barter agreements between the Soviet Union and its satellite states. The Council for Mutual Economic Assistance (COMECON), established in 1949, functioned as an economic organisation under Soviet leadership. Its purpose was to coordinate

---

[1] Statistical data are available on the website of the US Energy Information Administration (EIA): <http://www.eia.doe.gov/emeu/aer/petro.html (04/05/2024)>.

and facilitate the economic development of Eastern Bloc countries, including the Soviet Union, Bulgaria, Czechoslovakia, East Germany, Hungary, Poland, and Romania. Although ideologically positioned as a counterweight to capitalism, in practice, the CMEA often mirrored the West's economic growth patterns.

One tangible outcome of economic collaboration within the Soviet Bloc was the Friendship Pipeline (Druzhba), constructed in the 1960s, with its main sections completed between 1960 and 1964. Built by the Soviet Union, the pipeline transported crude oil from Soviet oil fields to various countries in Eastern and Central Europe. Its purpose was twofold: to strengthen economic ties between the Soviet Union and its allies by ensuring a steady oil supply and to provide a secure and reliable energy source, reducing reliance on oil imports from non-Soviet countries.

Although its significance has evolved due to shifts in the geopolitical landscape and energy markets, the pipeline remains an important energy source. Its strategic role became particularly evident following the Russia-Ukraine war in 2022, when disruptions to pipeline operations caused severe energy price increases in Central Europe. This, in turn, limited the region's ability to manoeuvre on key aspects of economic decarbonisation. While higher fossil fuel prices could accelerate the transition to cleaner energy, they also place significant financial strain on industries and households, requiring greater public and private resources that could otherwise be allocated elsewhere.

Between 1945 and 1973, the promise of an apparently unlimited supply of low-cost oil – both in the West and the East – contributed to widespread social and political insensitivity to ecological limits and an unwavering focus on economic expansion (Hobsbawm, 1994; Gould et al., 2004). This period marked a global transformation toward oil as the primary energy source, affecting not only industry and transportation but also agriculture. Cheap transportation costs, coupled with global inequalities and economic development, fuelled the growing consumption of natural resources.

The collapse of the CMEA in the early 1990s and the integration of formerly centrally planned economies into the capitalist system did little to alter this trajectory. Instead, it accelerated the shared economic and environmental challenges that both Western and Central European countries continue to face. Breaking this legacy requires overcoming deeply entrenched infrastructure and vested interests, a monumental task that demands viable and affordable alternatives.

The era of cheap oil is long gone, yet as we see today, even rising prices have not significantly reduced our dependence on fossil fuels. This is largely because alternative solutions in transport, heating, and industrial production have yet to become cheaper or more accessible. The challenge ahead lies in bridging this gap and making sustainable energy sources truly competitive.

1.3. Origins of European Environmental Policies

In December 1952, after a period of cold weather combined with an anticyclone and no wind, London was immersed in heavy smog for five days. This event became known as the Great Smog (or sometimes the Big Smog). It was just one in a series of industrial smog incidents that had begun to envelop the city with the rise of intensive industrial production. This phenomenon can even be found in the works of Charles Dickens and Arthur Conan Doyle, under lofty descriptions such as 'pea soup' or 'real London fog'. However, what these authors of colourful depictions could not have imagined were the consequences. According to Bell et al. (2004), the crisis in 1952 alone resulted in over 12,000 premature deaths due to the respiratory effects of smog on people exposed to air pollution. The fossil fuel-driven economic boom began generating increasing environmental consequences. Social problems followed, as the city experienced spatial development where wealthier elites moved to leeward locations, while poorer populations remained under the chimneys of factories, bearing the brunt of industrial pollution.

As science and technology progressed, the number of problems multiplied. Nuclear energy, initially a byproduct of military research, created one of the most controversial and costly issues: nuclear waste disposal. The chemical industry experienced a boom and turbulent development. The use of pesticides and herbicides revolutionised agriculture. The expansion of industrial production, along with both existing and emerging environmental impacts, gradually triggered a response in a society where more data and information were becoming available.

In the 1960s, a more radical confrontation emerged between the concept of economic growth and its critics from environmental and social perspectives.

One of the first eco-social critics of the system was Murray Bookchin, whose book *Our Synthetic Environment* was published in 1962. It is telling that Rachel Carson's *Silent Spring*, published six months later, attracted much greater media and public attention, despite being less radical and more nostalgic than Bookchin's work. While Carson exposed the negative impact of pesticide use, particularly DDT, and its effects on wildlife and human health, she did not delve deeply into the economic structures driving these issues. Nevertheless, Silent Spring is now remembered as a landmark event in the formation of the environmental movement and the political push for systematic environmental protection.

Topics such as ecology, health, and sustainability gradually emerged as legitimate concerns for policymakers. In the early decades following World War II, European nations were primarily focused on economic recovery and industrial expansion. Once post-war reconstruction was complete, society on both sides of the Iron Curtain began to question the cost of progress – more openly in the West, but also, surprisingly persistently, in the East.

The evolution of public debate reflected the changing economic and social landscape. Air pollution continued to worsen as industrial production increased. This period preceded the migration of industries to lower-wage countries, marking the time when Europe reached peak industrialisation. The German Ruhr region, northern Italy, and French industrial zones began experiencing the consequences of unchecked economic development.

The industrial zone in northern Italy, home to engineering and chemical industries, dealt with its waste problem by dumping industrial pollutants into the Venetian Lagoon, which connects the mainland to historic Venice. By the 1970s, pollution levels had reached alarming levels, and it took another 20 years to partially clean the lagoon and restore the ecosystem of this unique area. This and many other examples illustrate how environmental conditions in Western Europe were systematically deteriorating.

The amount of scientific information on pollution's impact on nature and human health was also increasing. Pressure from new social movements, combined with the direct risks to human populations, gradually led to national-level environmental reforms. The 1972 Seveso disaster in Italy, where a dioxin leak posed a massive health threat, reinforced the need for stronger environmental policies across Europe. Governments began regulating industrial emissions, and laws restricting uncontrolled waste disposal were enacted.

By the 1960s, growing public awareness of pollution and ecological degradation led to the first national environmental laws, particularly in countries like Germany, the Netherlands, and Sweden, which introduced early air and water pollution regulations. However, differences in national approaches led to regulatory disparities within the common market, causing trade tensions. Gradually, the European Economic Community (EEC) – which later became the European Union (EU) – began taking the initiative.

The roots of modern EU environmental policy can be traced back to the 1970s. Several key factors influenced its development. The most significant was likely the creation of the Single European Market, where environmental policies and national legislation varied in focus, goals, and regulatory intensity. This created unequal costs for industries and polluters, leading to tensions and favouring businesses from countries with less regulation and lower costs.

Another factor was public pressure from civil movements, as citizens – particularly in times of economic growth and social stability – became more inclined to support stronger environmental protections. Finally, there was the international context, including growing concerns about the global environment, as highlighted by the 1972 UN Conference on the Human Environment in Stockholm. These factors, combined with the EEC's growing ambitions, pushed environmental policy onto the European agenda.

The European Commission responded by introducing Environmental Action Programmes (EAPs), which remain the backbone of EU environmental policy today. The first EAP, adopted in November 1973, emphasised that economic development, prosperity, and environmental protection were interconnected and essential EEC objectives. Over time, these programmes evolved, shifting from a market-based focus to integrated, cross-sectoral strategies. The most recent, the eighth EAP, entered into force in 2022 and serves as the EU's environmental policy roadmap until 2030. This process culminated in the European Green Deal (2020), the most ambitious climate and environmental strategy in EU history.

The EU gradually emerged as a global leader in environmental policy, spearheading international environmental agreements. However, significant challenges remain. The primary challenge is global economic competition, where varying environmental standards make it difficult to balance sustainability with economic competitiveness. Another issue is the decline in political and public support, as governments and businesses increasingly frame environmental protection as a competitive disadvantage.

According to Schnaiberg (2009), this decline in environmental commitment must be analysed in the context of shifting economic dynamics. As globalisation has intensified, corporate influence has expanded, and capital has become more mobile, placing pressure on national governments to prioritise economic growth over environmental commitments. Hobsbawm (1994) describes the end of the post-war 'golden age' of capitalism (1950–1975), highlighting the shift toward market liberalisation and deregulation.

As the EU attempts to redefine environmental policy as a source of economic competitiveness, a critical question remains: Will environmental policy remain robust, promoting innovation and sustainability, or will it be undermined by short-term economic pressures? For now, policy-driven investments in clean technologies are expected to drive future economic growth, but neoliberal trends across Europe pose substantial obstacles. The path the EU ultimately chooses will determine whether it maintains its environmental leadership or retreats in response to economic pressures.

1.4. Planned Socialism and the Illusion of an Alternative

The alternative to capitalism began in the ruins of the Winter Palace in Saint Petersburg, Russia. It went through various ups and downs, only to collapse spectacularly during a live broadcast at the turn of the 1980s and 1990s. Some call it communism, state socialism, centrally planned directive socialism, or even state capitalism. For this book, we will use the term 'centrally planned socialism'. The state was both the actor and the target of an arrangement based on the social ownership of the means of production. The economy was controlled by the state and its apparatus, which was appointed and subsequently managed by communist parties. Yet, the paradox is that this alternative system was, from the very beginning, captive to the same system it defined itself against. Central Europe verbally distanced itself from capitalism in its economic policies but, in practice, copied the Western model of modernisation.

Even though centrally planned socialism was explicitly anti-capitalist, with the government controlling the economy, industries, and businesses, it still engaged in market-driven economic activities. Ideologically, it was built on the same foundation of economic growth through industrialisation as its Western counterparts. In the Soviet Union and later in Central and Eastern Europe, the success of industrialisation was measured in coal and steel production. This approach was not significantly different from early industrialisation in England or, later, South Korea. In *Green Political Thoughts*, Andrew Dobson (2000) describes both capitalism and centrally planned socialism (as practiced in the former Eastern Bloc, as well as in parts of Asia and Africa) as systems based on 'industrialism' – a commitment to economic growth and increasing consumption. The fundamental difference lay in the ownership of the means of production and the redistribution of profits.

Soviet industrialisation was based on the assumption that massive increases in production capacity would pave the way for a communist society. All resources – including natural ones – were to serve rapid industrial development. According to Walt Rostow (1960: 93), economic development in Russia in the 1960s was similar to that of the United States, except that Russia lagged behind by half a century in industrial production per capita. Rostow argued that institutions and government systems affect only the speed of industrialisation, not its trajectory.

Although Central European countries had been undergoing various forms of industrialisation since the 1870s, the process accelerated significantly once they were incorporated into centrally planned economies. The heavy industrialisation model introduced in the Soviet Union in the 1930s was adopted as a development paradigm in post-World War II socialist states.

After 1945, economic growth in Central Europe was primarily driven by industrial expansion. From the post-war low point, industrial output rebounded to pre-1939 levels by 1950 and continued to grow at a rapid pace over the next two decades, quickly outpacing other sectors of the economy. In Czechoslovakia and Hungary, industrial value added measured in constant prices doubled during the 1950s and tripled between 1950 and 1970 (Klein at al 2017). Inevitably, the boom in heavy industry had led to severe air and water pollution, particularly in heavily industrialised areas such as Silesia (Poland, Czech Republic), northern Slovakia, and northwestern Czech Republic.

The entire course of this industrialisation process followed a similar logic to that of non-socialist states, but with one remarkable feature: scale. As Alexander Gerschenkron (1962) argues, late-industrialising countries tend to experience rapid industrial growth, with pressure to create large industrial enterprises and state involvement in production and financing. Understanding this pattern of late industrialisation is crucial to analysing the structural challenges faced during the transition from central planning to a market economy in the 1990s.

Later industrialisation was characterised by the concentration of production, the construction of large industrial conglomerates, and the use of economies of scale. The state-controlled economy model, focused on heavy industry, dominated Central Europe, leading to massive investments in energy, steel, and manufacturing. Nuclear power plants, originally a byproduct of military research, were meant to secure energy resources, while the smokestacks of factories became symbols of progress.

While industrialisation in the West was driven by the interests of capital in collaboration with the state, in Central Europe, economic policy was determined by local communist parties under the supervision of the Soviet Union. The extent to which state policies reflected societal interests remains debatable, but it is clear that the state was never a neutral actor – neither in socialist nor capitalist development. The first post-war decades were, in many ways, a golden age for both centrally planned socialism and capitalism, with rising production, employment, wages, and living standards. Political repression in the East gradually eased.

Both economic systems encouraged industrial expansion, relying on energy-intensive processes and state support for business and industry. Environmental concerns were not a priority in the post-war period. Another crucial factor was the Cold War, in which heavy industry and armament production were seen as strategic investments.

For a time, Central Europe was able to keep pace with Western industrial development. However, from the 1960s onward, problems emerged. Historically, Central European countries had occupied a semi-peripheral position in Western Europe, but now they found themselves in a core position within the Soviet Bloc. This stimulated research and development and led to technological progress in East Germany and Czechoslovakia, but global competition – dominated by capitalist economies with access to global resources – left them at a disadvantage.

The closed nature of the Eastern Bloc forced Central European countries to rely on domestic resources and state-led industrial policies. Unlike the West, which outsourced polluting industries to developing countries, socialist economies bore the full brunt of their own environmental degradation. A case in point is nickel production: while Western economies relied on nickel mining in New Caledonia, leaving local populations to suffer the environmental consequences, the Eastern Bloc polluted its own regions, as seen in Sered, Slovakia.

The nickel smelter in Sered remains a symbol of environmental devastation, illustrating the prioritisation of self-sufficiency over sustainability. With the end of central planning, market conditions rendered many heavy industries unprofitable, leading to their collapse in the 1990s. However, the legacy of these industries, including pollution and unemployment, still shapes contemporary climate and energy debates.

By the 1970s, Central Europe's technological lag was evident, including in environmental protection. Western Europe, pressured by public opinion and environmental policies, developed cleaner technologies – forcing socialist countries to import them at high costs. This bureaucratic and financial burden further slowed environmental progress.

The debate over climate change today echoes past ideological divisions. As Tom Tietenberg (1992: 46) notes, some Western economists in the 1970s believed that centralised economies could better manage environmental challenges, while dissidents in socialist states argued that capitalism provided better solutions.

In reality, the form of ownership was less decisive than the political and economic structures governing decision-making. The environmental degradation of post-war Europe was a result of industrialisation, affecting both East and West, and continues to shape today's decarbonisation efforts.

By the 1980s, environmental issues contributed to political unrest in Central Europe. Mass protests in northern Bohemia and demonstrations against the Gabcikovo-Nagymaros dam project were early signs of public dissent. The deteriorating environment, combined with economic stagnation and political repression, ultimately weakened the regimes and contributed to their collapse in 1989.

1.5. Back to the 'Normal'?

One of the popular clichés deeply embedded in public debate in Central Europe is the idea that current environmental problems are the 'legacy' of communism. In reality, the issue is far more complex. Environmental problems are not solely the result of 40 years of attempts at an alternative system, though the former regime bears significant responsibility for the severe environmental degradation it left behind.

The so-called 'Black Triangle' is located on the border of Germany, the Czech Republic, and Poland. In the years before political changes in all three countries, this region was synonymous with pollution, environmental devastation, and smog alarms. The main source of pollution was sulphur dioxide emissions from nearby brown coal power plants. As Philip Sarre and Peter Jehlička (2007) describe, the situation became so unbearable that, even before the mass protests in Prague in November 1989, it sparked early demonstrations against social conditions in the region. These protests foreshadowed the eventual collapse of the regime.

Thirty years later, the situation has changed dramatically. The decline of brown coal mining and the modernisation of power plants led to fundamental improvements. Air quality has improved, and nature is gradually regenerating. On the other hand, job losses were significant. According to data from the Teplice Labour Office, two decades later, out of twenty-three major employers in the district in 1991, only five remained, and their 5,129 employees represented only one-fifth of the original workforce.

One of the defining images of the changing Central European landscape became crumbling factories – relics of past industrialisation. What took decades in the United States and Western Europe happened within just a few years in Central Europe. Entire industries collapsed not necessarily because they were unable to produce, but because they lacked marketing strategies, financial know-how, and the ability to compete. The markets were soon flooded with foreign competition.

American sociology has studied deindustrialisation since the 1970s, focusing on its social and economic impacts (Jefferson and Heathcott 2003, High and Lewis 2007). The Rust Belt – stretching from the northeastern United States through Pennsylvania, Ohio, Indiana, and Michigan – became the archetypal deindustrialised region, filled with abandoned factories and economic decline. Once thriving industrial hubs in England and the Rhineland met a similar fate, as mines and foundries closed and industrial buildings were repurposed into hotels, apartments, or cultural centres.

In the United States and Western Europe, these changes occurred gradually and during times of economic growth. Even so, the transition came at a high economic and social cost. In Central Europe, by contrast, reforms were dramatically rapid. Combined with an unprecedented shift in ownership structures and a lack of transparency, this often led to unclear accountability for old environmental burdens. The immediate environmental and social impacts were undeniable.

The disintegration of the Soviet Bloc and the abrupt transition from a centrally planned socialist economy triggered a profound economic crisis across Central Europe. The early 1990s were marked by dramatic declines in industrial output, rising unemployment, and a collapse in traditional trade networks, particularly those tied to the Council for Mutual Economic Assistance (Comecon). This systemic shock resulted not only in economic contraction but also in deep social and political upheaval, as countries struggled to restructure their economies amid institutional vacuum and European and global competitive pressures.

Between 1987 and 1992, industrial production declined by 37 % and 28 % in in Czechoslovakia and Hungary (Klein at al 2017). The early years of the economic transition from central planning to a market economy in Central Europe led to significant economic contractions, including the collapse of many factories and entire industries. In 1991, the GDP of the Czech lands, then part of Czechoslovakia, fell by 11.6 %. By 1997, the Czech Republic's GDP remained more than 9 % below its 1989 level, while in Slovakia, GDP plummeted by a record 14.57 % in 1991, and it wasn't until 2007 that GDP per capita surpassed 1989 levels (Turnovec 1998).

The economic downturn, driven by the deindustrialisation of entire regions, inevitably led to improvements in environmental indicators. For example, carbon dioxide emissions per capita, which in 1989 were 16.8 tons in the Czech Republic and 11.1 tons in Slovakia, dropped to 11 tons in the Czech Republic and 7.4 tons in Slovakia by 1999. However, improvements in air and water quality were often associated with inflation, unemployment, and economic uncertainty – themes that resonate today in discussions about decarbonisation.

The old economic system collapsed, and its successor became the centre of debate about the future of the welfare state. At the same time, neoliberal economic theory, deeply influenced by British Prime Minister Margaret Thatcher and American President Ronald Reagan, was becoming dominant in the West. Many Central European countries placed their bets on shock therapy, embracing radical market liberalisation.

The collapse of the centrally planned system was not just a sudden event but the culmination of long-term decay. In many former industrial hubs, this was followed by a new phase of decline, driven by neoliberal reforms of the early 1990s. High hopes failed to materialise for many, and this deepened the roots of today's political landscape. Two of the strongest illusions of the period were belief in a quick and smooth transition and faith in the power of civil society.

Although each Central European country had its own unique path, certain common trends emerged. The late 1980s and early 1990s led to a complete transformation of ownership relations and a transition to market capitalism. The system was rapidly deregulated and opened to international competition. However, little attention was paid to the fact that many people lacked the knowledge and experience to navigate the new economic environment.

Even though centrally planned socialism had, in its final decades, experimented with limited market mechanisms, the transition to capitalism was far from easy. Adding to the complexity, the Western core economies were no longer the strong welfare states of the 1960s and 1970s but were themselves undergoing neoliberal transformation.

The changes in Central Europe after 1989 were essentially an accelerated version of the processes that had already begun in the West a decade earlier – deregulation, privatisation, and outsourcing, all accompanied by a decline in industrial production. Combined with weak political and managerial structures, this led to the deindustrialisation of entire regions, as seen in Hungary and Poland, or even near-complete deindustrialisation, as in Bulgaria.

The mass collapse of industrial enterprises – once the backbone of regional economies – was rapid and painful. Thousands of skilled workers were left jobless, and mass migration to the West became a common survival strategy. In the absence of a strong political left, many voters shifted toward right-wing and ultra-right parties.

Even though the former system collapsed from above, its domestic opponents and critics actively contributed to widening its cracks. Among them, the green movement played a pivotal role. However, just as it gained influence before 1989, it lost relevance just as quickly afterward. The green movement of the late 1980s often contained a strong narrative of creating a third way – a socio-environmental alternative between socialism and capitalism.

In the immediate aftermath of 1989, environmental concerns were widely discussed, topping public opinion polls. However, just a few years later, environmental issues lost public support in Eastern Europe (Pickvance 1999, McCormick 2001, Schnaiberg 2009). The new economic reality forced people to shift their priorities – salaries and employment became more pressing than environmental protection. The idea of balancing economic growth with environmental and social goals was soon dismissed by new elites as utopian.

In hindsight, the push for an alternative socio-economic model was like a fight between David and Goliath. However, in modern society, David only wins when social and economic conditions allow it. That was not the case in Central Europe after 1989. Instead, new regimes became even more rigidly committed to deregulation, growth, and consumption than many Western counterparts.

While environmental indicators improved, social and economic conditions deteriorated in the 1990s. In the absence of a shared vision, the main goal became integration with the West – militarily into NATO, economically into the European Union. The dominant illusion became the dream of a better life elsewhere, embodied in the popular slogan 'going back to Europe'.

1.6. The Disappearing Vision of the European Union

Europe has traversed a complex path over the past century. It has been the site of multiple waves of industrialisation, various models of democracy and welfare states, as well as an arena for ideological experiments, from fascism and post-fascist regimes in the South to centrally planned socialism in the East. The lines of these divisions are still visible today. While the history of European integration can be traced back to various treaties and alliances, deeper cooperation only began in the twentieth century, with true pan-European integration occurring after the collapse of the Berlin Wall in 1989. A significant milestone in this evolution was the European Coal and Steel Community, the first major European institution established after World War II to integrate coal and steel industries into a common market based on supranationalism. Paradoxically, the foundations of the European Union were built on fossil fuels.

By 1960, unemployment in Great Britain was 1.5%, and in West Germany, it was around 1% (Harman 2008: 548). This period is often referred to as the golden age of capitalism (Hobsbawm 1994, Braudel 1993, Arrighi 1994, 2000). People increasingly felt confident that they would find employment, have access to affordable healthcare, and benefit from social security in times of need or old age. A new post-war generation was coming of age, and higher education was becoming more accessible.

The post-war economic boom led to considerable economic and social progress, strengthening the welfare state, largely as a result of global competition between two ideological systems. Within this context, we must also examine the structural conditions that led to the emergence of the green movement, the development of green politics, and the image of the European Union as an island of prosperity and well-being.

In 1993, the European Union was formally established when the Maastricht Treaty came into force. In 2004, the EU expanded to include former socialist countries, with Poland, Hungary, the Czech Republic, and Slovakia joining. The long-standing vision of 'joining Europe', which dominated public discourse in Central Europe from the early 1990s, became a reality. These countries fully adopted EU environmental and climate legislation, although transitional periods were negotiated for implementing cost-intensive regulations. EU cohesion policy and investment flows were prioritised for climate and environmental measures.

It was a challenging period for Central European administrations. The European Union's environmental and climate policies constitute a complex system of legislation and measures that are binding on its member states (Barnes and Barnes 1999, Jordan 2005). There is ongoing debate as to whether this framework is primarily driven by efforts to prevent disruptions to the common market and economic interests or whether it is the result of public pressure and the collective will of EU citizens and member states. What is clear is that EU expansion had profound and far-reaching effects, and the prospect of EU membership played a crucial role in advancing environmental policies in aspiring countries (Andonova 2004, Andonova et al. 2005, Auer 2004, Jordan 2005).

The early conflicts over environmental policy, which were visible even during the pre-accession period, persist today. According to Andonova (2004), the economic interests of businesses significantly influenced how Central European countries approached different aspects of EU environmental legislation. For instance, in the chemical industry, which is predominantly oriented toward European markets, it was in the industry's interest to quickly adapt to EU standards. In contrast, energy production, which is more focused on domestic markets, made the process of air protection legislation reform more difficult. Biodiversity protection and the designation of protected areas became major battlegrounds involving landowners, developers, conservationists, and the public.

Despite these challenges, the overhaul of the legislative framework for climate and environmental policy resulted in substantial improvements. Within a few years, these countries had to implement policies that were highly complex and had taken decades to develop in the EU. In retrospect, it was a massive modernisation project, and without the influence and pressure of the EU, many progressive steps in nature conservation would likely never have taken place.

Three decades after enlargement, it is clear that EU climate and environmental policies have had a positive impact on Central Europe. However, it is also evident that while these countries remain both subjects and objects of policy-making, their roles and attitudes have evolved.

With some simplification, we can say that the stronger and 'greener' the attitudes of individual member states, the stronger the EU's environmental policy becomes. This is because the final policies often reflect the smallest common denominator among member states' interests. Central Europe's positions and attitudes toward climate and environmental policies have inevitably shifted – both positively and negatively.

From being a passive recipient of policies shaped by other countries, Central Europe has moved to the centre of these processes and has become a co-creator. Early analyses by Skjaerseth and Wettestad (2007) pointed out that, contrary to pessimistic predictions, EU enlargement did not weaken environmental policy. Instead, they found different effects across three key areas: it increased pressure to regulate genetically modified crops, weakened the implementation of the Emissions Trading Directive, and had little impact on air protection policies.

One advantage of EU membership is that the legal framework limits excesses and provides a safeguard against national lobbying interests. This is particularly important for smaller states, which often have weaker administrative capacities and political instability. For example, in 2011, Slovakia was involved in seventeen proceedings initiated by the EU due to violations of environmental legislation, forcing the country to quickly amend its laws. The EU's legally binding framework creates a barrier against arbitrary national legal changes, which are sometimes driven by local lobbyist groups.

It became apparent that the main climate policy tensions in Central Europe crystallise around energy and industrial interests. Poland, and to some extent the Czech Republic, heavily depend on coal. Meanwhile, Hungary and Slovakia continue to host heavy, material- and energy-intensive industries. While part of this industry collapsed in the 1990s, some survived, such as iron mills in Ostrava (Czech Republic), Katowice (Poland), and Košice (Slovakia).

This industrial concentration increased in the 2000s as part of a manufacturing shift from higher-wage countries to lower-cost economies. Here, multinational corporate interests often clash with the costs associated with climate policies. The early discourse in Central Europe about adopting EU policies was soon overshadowed by economic concerns.

The European Union has become the main modernisation force in Central Europe, setting the pace for market integration and decarbonisation with the European Green Deal and its 2050 climate neutrality goal. However, many member states are losing momentum. There is strong political pressure to slow down climate and environmental policies, yet no clear vision for what comes next. Market transformation in Central Europe is essentially complete, but these countries now face global challenges as part of the EU, grappling with new dilemmas and decisions.

From a historical perspective, it can be said that Central European countries, once semi-peripheral to Western capitalism, have returned to the forefront after a 40-year detour. They have benefitted from the EU's modernisation project but now realise that the challenges faced by core economies are also their challenges. Their high dependence as producers of semi-products for Western manufacturers makes them vulnerable. The Czech Republic, sometimes called Germany's backup engine, and other Central European economies are immediately affected when Western car manufacturers face competition from China.

The European Green Deal, adopted during a period of economic optimism, envisions a sustainable, climate-secure, and socially just Europe. However, the post-COVID 19 and post-Russian invasion economic landscape has led to rising tensions. The vision of an ever-growing, prosperous Europe is showing cracks, and while the Green Deal remains a plan, its effectiveness and political support remain uncertain.

1.7. Capitalism as the Winning System

There were initially diverse perspectives on how to economically reorganise society after the political changes and the collapse of centrally planned socialism. A famous quote from Václav Havel (1989) captures this transition: *'For twenty years, official propaganda claimed that I was an enemy of socialism, that I wanted to restore capitalism in our country... It was all lies.'*

Despite early debates and alternative visions for transformation in Central Europe, the transition quickly gravitated toward free-market capitalism. While there were nuances between countries and varying speeds of change, nearly all veered away from social market capitalism, opting instead for more or less neoliberal economic transformations.

Once the initial wave of privatisation settled, a new economic system took shape, gaining support from emerging industrial owners and managers. These new elites, increasingly interwoven with media and think tanks they helped finance, reinforced the dominance of capital. Capitalism emerged as the clear winner in Central Europe – and beyond. As Branko Milanović (2019) argues in his book *Capitalism, Alone*: *'We are all capitalists now.'* For the first time in human history, the world is dominated by a single economic system.

There is perhaps no better theoretical foundation to analyse the contradictions of capitalism than through the works of the classics. Karl Marx's works and the school he created remain relevant when applied to the analysis of capitalist society, particularly in the context of climate change. This includes understanding how the positive and negative externalities of production are distributed and how society resolves the contradictions between labour, surplus value, and the environment.

Marx's original works are based on the premise of industrial development. He sees growth as the foundation for producing resources and improving the lives of workers. The pathway to this was a revolutionary change in the ownership of the means of production. He developed a theory about the 'metabolic rift' of the expansion of the capitalist mode of production and the weakening of the link between humans and nature (from which humans derive their basic resources). However, his main theses did not address environmental aspects directly, and it's not surprising.

Given the nineteenth-century context of knowledge in which he wrote, there was little understanding of the wider causal links between industrialisation and its environmental effects. Marx viewed these primarily within the economic and social spheres. Over time, however, his analyses and conclusions have been applied to understanding environmental problems, with climate change now being the principal issue. In this regard, we can particularly draw from the works of James O'Connor and Bellamy Foster.

Foster mainly focuses on the critical analysis of the mechanisms by which the capitalist mode of production inevitably leads to environmental destruction (Foster 2002, 2010). In this perspective, he builds on James O'Connor (1988: 11), who formulated two key contradictions of capitalism, seen as the main reasons why a more radical positive ecological change cannot occur within the system.

The first contradiction is related to the fact that the rate of resource utilisation is both a sociological and an economic category. Capital holds social and political power over labour, but it also faces the inherent problem of creating a crisis due to overproduction. If capital puts too much pressure on labour costs, profitability increases, but it also raises the risk of overproduction crises. Therefore, capital must constantly innovate, create new products, and develop systems of loans, leasing, and marketing tools. Increasing sales is a must. This leads to pressure on natural resources, waste, and environmental destruction. Alan Schnaiberg and his followers further developed this idea in the treadmill theory, which we discuss later in the book (Schnaiberg 1980, Gould et al. 2004).

O'Connor's second contradiction, which has significant environmental implications, involves capitalism's self-destructive adaptation and exploitation of labour, urban infrastructure, space, and environmental externalities. He calls it 'self-destructive' because the costs of health, education, urban transport, private or commercial rents, and the extraction of resources from nature eventually turn into social costs (O'Connor, 1988). In other words, the less the external costs of production (such as economic and social impacts of climate change) are reflected in the price of the product, the more profitable the producer becomes. The ultimate result is a 'self-destructive' tendency.

The fundamental interest of capital is to resist any progress toward internalising environmental or social costs, as well as to avoid reflecting externalities from production and consumption that could negatively impact profitability. However, this does not mean that these costs will not rise over time – partly as a societal response to capitalism's self-destructive tendencies, and partly because new regulatory frameworks can create new products and markets. Changes within capitalism are therefore possible, even when they contradict the system's core drive for profit maximisation. However, such changes face strong resistance and are typically only accepted when they also generate profit.

When the EU's common environmental policy was introduced in the 1970s – primarily as a prerequisite for the creation of a single economic space and common market – it appeared that gradual regulations and standards could successfully mitigate the environmental impact of capital. However, in classical Marxist theory, such reforms remain partial and fail to address the fundamental contradictions of the system, which is why they eventually face structural limitations.

Moreover, the EU operates within an increasingly globalised economic framework, making it an open economic space subject to external competition. Initially, the EU championed openness as a flagship policy, but as it began to face intensifying competition – particularly from China – the notion of strategic autonomy gained prominence.

From a Marxist perspective, any attempt to introduce deeper systemic change within capitalist society is ultimately doomed to failure because the logic of capital and the imperatives of environmental protection are structurally antagonistic. Existing policy solutions tend to have limited impact, and substantial change will only occur when there is a radical reassessment of ownership structures, resource allocation, and the governance of production – effectively challenging the core principles on which capitalist economies function.

To take truly meaningful and effective steps in tackling climate change, a coordinated global restructuring of the world's energy, agricultural, and transport systems would be necessary – alongside compensation mechanisms for those most affected by the transition. However, such a cohesive effort is virtually impossible in a fragmented and competitive global economy. In the absence of common international action, the only viable alternative lies in the gradual greening of capitalist economies, driven by a mix of global and regional agreements, as well as the market interests of multinational corporations and domestic businesses.

This assumption is based on the premise that green investments can be accommodated by capitalism, but only if they generate profit. According to David Harvey (2010, 2018), a fundamental feature of capitalism is its need for perpetual growth. Due to the competitive nature of capitalist markets, businesses must continuously innovate, expand, and seek new markets to maintain an advantage. The pressure to maximise profit compels firms to reinvest their earnings into production, infrastructure, and technology. Without constant expansion, businesses risk stagnation, falling behind competitors, or being acquired. In this framework, capitalism requires compound growth to sustain itself, meaning it must expand exponentially over time.

The dynamics of economic growth, production levels, and innovation shape the global geopolitical landscape, determining which nations or blocs dominate the international order. Harvey's critique of capitalism highlights how its structural imperatives – including competition, overaccumulation, and the falling rate of profit – fuel an endless cycle of expansion and crisis (Harvey 2010). This raises critical questions about capitalism's long-term sustainability, particularly in the face of climate change and resource depletion. After all, limitless economic growth is fundamentally incompatible with the finite resources of the planet.

Capitalism is not just about producing goods and services – it is about the expansion of capital itself. This relentless drive for accumulation influences economic, social, and environmental dynamics, shaping globalisation, financialisation, and ecological destruction.

Capitalism survives through a cycle of creative destruction – constantly phasing out outdated industries while creating new ones to revitalise the system. One of the great illusions we face is the belief that capital accumulation can be seamlessly redirected toward productive investments in electric vehicles, renewable energy, or solar panels. However, for sustainable investments to surpass and replace carbon-intensive industries, the cost structures must be fundamentally restructured – including the internalisation of both positive and negative externalities – and a complete shift in policy incentives and subsidies would be necessary.

This process would not only have to absorb surplus capital, but it would also have to temporarily resolve problems of overaccumulation by opening new fields of investment. However, the 'new' economy requires strong policy frameworks and subsidies to level the playing field – allowing green industries to scale up and compete with the entrenched 'old' economy. In turn, such policies demand public support.

As we argue in the next section, an increasing number of climate-related drivers are enabling political and economic backing for green investments. It is not that capitalism cannot generate transition – it can. But the pace of change is too slow, and much of the progress is offset by rising global consumption and the increasing homogenisation of consumption patterns across continents. Ultimately, the challenge remains: can capitalism reinvent itself fast enough to avert its own environmental collapse?

Europe and Climate Change: Drivers and Outlook

Article 2 of the UN Framework Convention on Climate Change defines the primary goal of climate policies: to stabilise greenhouse gas concentrations at a level that prevents dangerous anthropogenic impacts on the climate system. However, this very definition raises fundamental questions: What constitutes a 'safe level'? What happens if global temperatures rise beyond the widely accepted thresholds of 1.5 or 2 degrees Celsius? Despite numerous efforts and declarations, current trends suggest that these limits will be breached.

This leads to critical questions, both globally and particularly for Europe: What policies, legislative steps, and programmes are necessary? What actions are possible? And ultimately, who will bear the cost?

It is useful to view these trends in the context of the global economy. US funding for climate initiatives increased from $1.5 billion in FY 2021 to $5.8 billion in FY 2022. Projections suggest a compound annual growth rate of 22.1% for the US green technology and sustainability market from 2024 to 2030 (HD, 2025). While political shifts, such as the 2024 US presidential elections and potential withdrawal from the Paris Agreement, may alter trajectories, the transition is already underway and cannot be easily reversed.

Similarly, China invested $890 billion in clean energy sectors in 2023 – equivalent to the GDP of Switzerland or Turkey – with output growth reaching 30% year-on-year. China's ambition is to lead the world in green technology and services as part of the low-carbon transition. Are we on the brink of a global green transformation? The answer is yes, but the problem lies in the speed of change and its uneven geographical distribution.

The consensus on the anthropogenic causes and severe consequences of climate change has strongly influenced EU policies, leading to notable progress but also persistent resistance. Despite the systemic constraints, there is still political will and room for further action. Alongside opposition to climate neutrality goals, there is also growing pressure for more aggressive action.

Climate change is no longer a distant or hypothetical problem – it is a pressing reality. Europe, in fact, is the fastest-warming continent in the world (EEA, 2024). Despite efforts to slow temperature increases, the goals of the Paris Agreement are unlikely to be met (IPCC, 2019). According to increasingly realistic scenarios, global temperatures could rise by at least 2°C between 2040 and 2060 (IPCC, 2021, 2022, 2023). Pessimistic projections estimate that Europe may experience an average warming of at least 3°C over the next 50 years, with profound and far-reaching impacts on ecosystems, societies, and economies worldwide.

The European Union has officially declared climate change a political priority. Its decarbonisation policies, guided by the Paris Agreement and the European Green Deal, aim for carbon neutrality by 2050. According to the Green Deal, mobilising private investment and industry is essential. The plan envisions a 25-year transformation of Europe's industrial sector and entire value chains, supported financially by both EU and national governments through targeted financial schemes. This approach has accelerated decarbonisation, particularly through the phasing out of coal mining and the transformation of carbon-intensive industries.

The EU's share of global greenhouse gas emissions fell from 15.2% in 1990 to 7.3% in 2021, yet it remained the third-largest emitter, behind China and the United States. By 2020, the EU had aimed to reduce greenhouse gas emissions by 20% compared to 1990 levels, increase renewable energy's share to 20% of total energy consumption, and improve energy efficiency by 20%. The results exceeded these targets. Greenhouse gas emissions were reduced by approximately 24%, renewable energy reached 20%, and significant progress was made in energy efficiency (European Court of Auditors, 2024).

However, achieving further reductions toward the 2030, 2040, and 2050 targets will become increasingly costly. The 'low-hanging fruit' of cheaper solutions is gone. In Central Europe, the deindustrialisation and restructuring of the 1990s resulted in significant emissions reductions. Now, the focus must shift to households and transport – both extremely sensitive and politically vulnerable sectors.

Meanwhile, as global emissions continue to rise due to countries adopting capitalist development models, some voices argue that Europe has done enough. While Europe has made considerable progress, it is far from exhausting its potential, even when considering the structural constraints capitalism places on production and consumption patterns.

The EU's strategies to address climate change focus on replacing fossil fuels with renewable energy, embedding production within circular economic systems, and dematerialising consumption.

Positive trends in fossil fuel consumption have emerged, particularly following the Russia-Ukraine war and the disconnection from Russian gas and oil. In the first half of 2024, fossil fuel generation decreased by 17% compared to the same period in 2023 (-71 TWh), while demand grew by 0.7% (+9 TWh). As a result, fossil fuels accounted for just 27% of total EU electricity generation, down from 33% in 2023 (Graham & Fulghum, 2024).

Jean Pisani-Ferry and Simone Tagliapietra (2024) estimate that the EU will need to invest up to €1.3 trillion annually until 2030 and €1.54 trillion annually until 2050 to achieve climate neutrality. Such investments are unimaginable without higher taxes, subsidies, and national green investment strategies prioritising the transition.

These decisions lie largely in the hands of member states, whose economies are historically built on fossil-fuel-driven growth. For Central European countries, which rely on cheap labour, low taxes, and free capital flows, this presents an unsolvable puzzle.

The subordination of the environment and human well-being to the demands of capital accumulation creates a structural barrier to stronger climate policies. In the absence of robust systemic reforms, the prevailing narrative frames climate challenges as temporary hurdles – problems that can be solved through technological innovation. In typical capitalist fashion, it is often easier to invest in carbon capture and storage than to start a debate about profit taxation.

Nicholas Stern's groundbreaking *Stern Review on the Economics of Climate Change* (2006) frames climate change as the greatest market failure in history. Stern proposes solutions such as improving information flows, pricing carbon through taxation or regulation, and compensating those affected by climate-related impacts.

These ideas now form the basis of mainstream climate policy in Europe. Yet, one must ask: Is climate change merely a market failure, or is it a symptom of deeper systemic contradictions inherent in the global economic system?

The fundamental problem lies in the contradictions of capitalism. Economic growth and consumption are tightly intertwined with fossil fuel dependence, making it difficult to decouple economic expansion from greenhouse gas emissions. Europe is decarbonising, but often at the cost of importing emissions through outsourced products and services.

The relentless demand for growth, driven by capital accumulation, limits the scope for transformative policies. Without systemic change, we are expected to believe that incremental adjustments and technological fixes will suffice. Stern's market-based framing – emphasising carbon pricing and efficiency improvements – fails to confront the root causes of environmental degradation: the prioritisation of short-term profits over long-term sustainability.

While gradual progress has been made, current efforts are insufficient, partly due to the broader systemic context. Climate change is not just a technical or market-based problem – it is a symptom of deeper global contradictions. A truly transformative approach would require rethinking the economic structures and priorities that drive environmental degradation on a planetary scale.

Despite external pressures and internal resistance, climate change remains central to EU policy. Even with growing attacks on the Green Deal – not limited to Central Europe – the goal of European climate neutrality by 2050 remains alive, at least for now.

However, this path is increasingly shaped by a mix of ecological modernisation and neoliberal reforms – fuelled by the belief that economic growth can continue while reducing emissions through market efficiency and technological innovation. Climate change is treated more as a technical challenge than as an existential threat to the system itself.

Despite these challenges, there is still room for action. Every degree of warming prevented translates into significant economic and social savings. The urgency of the crisis demands a broader, more ambitious response, and Europe may yet serve as a laboratory to explore the limits of the current system.

2.1. A Chain Is Only as Strong as Its Weakest Link

European climate policy development is driven, on the one hand, by the realities of progressing climate change and its current or anticipated costs. It results from coordination with international bodies such as the United Nations Framework Convention on Climate Change (UNFCCC), aligning EU policies with global standards and commitments like the Paris Agreement. Yet it also reflects public sentiment and perceptions, often shaped by economic indicators. Ultimately, EU climate policy is a compromise – balancing geopolitical and domestic tensions, ambitions, and pressures from key stakeholders.

The EU's institutional and decision-making framework involves multiple layers of interaction among the European Commission, the European Parliament, and the Council of the EU, along with negotiations with individual member states and stakeholders. This consensus-seeking process often results in agreements based on the least common denominator. However, there are cases, such as the Green Deal, where high ambitions initially prevail, only to face resistance later when countries realise the scale and impact of the measures they have agreed upon.

In early 2025, the Polish Prime Minister criticised climate measures previously adopted by his own country, stating: *'We need a deep reflection on the potential rapid introduction of ETS2. I would really like to warn you against this move. I have some experience. You can believe me. The political impact is terribly predictable. It will have a very bad, disastrous political impact if energy prices continue to rise'* (Tusk, 2025).

What changed between the adoption of ETS2 and Donald Tusk's warning is perhaps the fact that, by 2025, energy prices in Europe were already three to four times higher than in the United States, not to mention China.

Central European countries entered the EU by adopting a comprehensive policy framework and legal package of strategies, treaties, and laws developed prior to their full EU membership in 2004. Since then, all measures have been co-created with their more or less active participation, but compromises remain necessary.

There are two fundamental challenges to reducing greenhouse gas emissions in the EU. First, any reduction imposes costs and directly affects key economic sectors, including energy, industry, and agriculture, with potential impacts on competitiveness. Second, due to the differing histories and economic trajectories of member states, these impacts are not evenly distributed, affecting countries and populations in diverse ways. Central Europe, with its history of industrialisation, recent concentration of energy-intensive manufacturing industries, lower income levels, and higher social inequalities, is particularly vulnerable.

Progress toward climate neutrality thus elicits both positive and negative reactions from diverse groups, each playing crucial roles in shaping, implementing, and influencing climate policies. Stakeholders involved in EU climate policy development are diverse, representing various sectors and interests. Their positions reflect the shifting opinions of the public in individual member states, influenced by vested interests or ideological commitments to certain development models – whether neoliberalisation or the welfare state (see Figure 4).

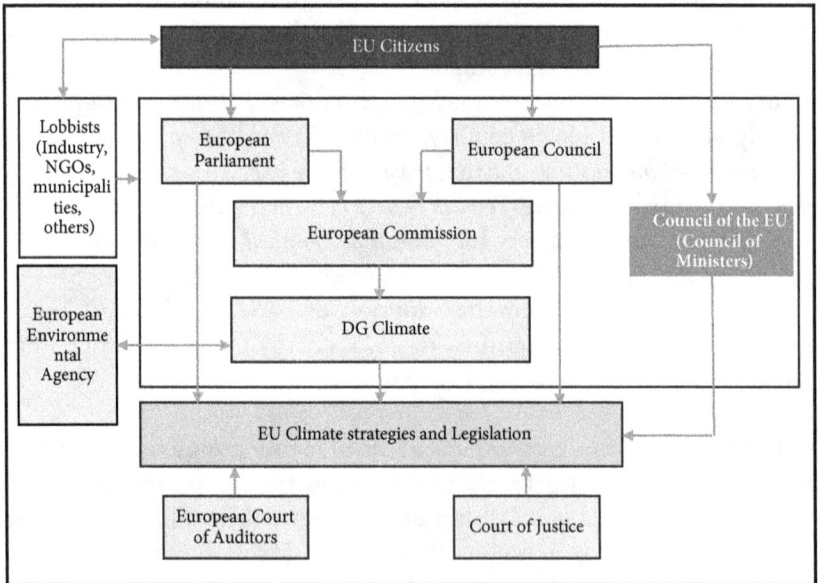

Figure 4: Schematic illustration of climate policy-making in the EU.
Source: The author.

The central role in the EU's climate policy-making system is played by the European institutions, particularly the European Commission. The Commission drives the legislative agenda on climate policies, sets targets, proposes regulations, and oversees their implementation. Within the Commission, the Directorate-General for Climate Action (DG CLIMA) is especially active. Although its role is theoretically impartial and technocratic, it is inevitably shaped by political perspectives and beliefs. Supporting this framework is the European Environment Agency (EEA), which provides essential data, indicators, and evidence-based monitoring, evaluation, and recommendations that inform the process.

The European Parliament plays a crucial role in policy-making. Members of the European Parliament (MEPs) promote and vote on climate measures, represent EU citizens, and provide input and amendments to climate legislation. However, political perspectives and the real or perceived impacts of climate policies on their constituencies significantly influence their decisions. Although MEPs theoretically represent all Europeans, they are elected by national voters, whose interests and perceptions of climate change often vary. For example, Poland, heavily reliant on coal energy and manufacturing industries, may have very different priorities from the Netherlands, which faces rising costs linked to climate adaptation investments, such as dike construction.

The European Council and the Council of the European Union are the primary bodies representing member states' interests. National governments negotiate and adopt climate legislation through ministers responsible for climate, energy, or economic policies. At the national level, these governments play a pivotal role in forming and implementing climate policies, often reflecting their unique economic structures, energy dependencies, and environmental priorities.

The EU's institutional framework and member states are subject to multi-layered lobbying at both the national level and in Brussels. These efforts primarily focus on promoting the interests of capital but, to some extent, also reflect the concerns of citizens – especially when these align with business interests. According to the Corporate Europe Observatory, there were an estimated 25,000 lobbyists working in Brussels in 2024, most representing the interests of corporations and their lobby groups.

Private sector and industry associations represent a wide array of interests in climate policy. These include renewable energy companies, fossil fuel industries, utility providers, and energy-intensive industries, which lobby for policies aligned with their business interests. These stakeholders are central to discussions about transitioning to a low-carbon economy. Agricultural organisations are likewise affected by regulations on emissions and land use. The push for carbon neutrality has also placed the automotive and transportation sectors at the forefront of adapting to stricter emissions standards and new technologies.

On the other side of the debate are environmental NGOs and advocacy groups, such as Greenpeace, WWF, Friends of the Earth, and the Club of Rome. These organisations advocate for stronger climate action, transparency, and ambitious targets. They provide scientific data, raise public awareness, and hold policymakers accountable. Think tanks, universities, and research institutions further contribute by conducting studies, offering data, and providing insights into the impacts of climate change and the effectiveness of policy measures. Public interest groups, including youth movements like Fridays for Future, have also emerged as significant players, mobilising public opinion and influencing climate discourse.

Municipalities, regional governments, and associations like the European Committee of the Regions play a vital role. They are often directly responsible for implementing policies on the ground, such as sustainable transport, urban planning, and waste management. Over the years, many active municipalities have benefitted significantly from European climate policies and funding initiatives.

Financial institutions and trade unions occupy a middle ground, with positions often shifting based on the perceived or real impacts of proposed measures. Trade unions and worker associations focus on the social and economic implications of climate policies, increasingly advocating for a 'just transition' to ensure workers are not disproportionately affected and that retraining opportunities exist for green economy jobs.

Banks, investment funds, and financial institutions are gradually aligning with sustainable finance initiatives and green investments. However, their main concern is the need for clear, transparent regulations to guide capital allocation toward climate-friendly projects. At the same time, many financial institutions continue to benefit from fossil fuel-based businesses, leading to ambiguity in their positions.

All in all, the EU's climate policy exists at the intersection of competing interests, with stakeholders influencing outcomes through lobbying, consultations, collaborations, and public advocacy. Policy outcomes are often shaped by broader economic trends, inflation, and development prospects – or the lack thereof. In 2019, when the European Green Deal was adopted, the mood was characterised by economic growth and perceived security. However, just five years later, the discourse has shifted dramatically due to COVID-19, inflation, the war in Ukraine, and the rapid economic rise of China. This shift has redirected the focus toward protectionism and security.

Central European countries often lack a unified political vision or consensus across the political spectrum on the essential principles and needs of the green transformation. Instead, decarbonisation is frequently framed in opposition to 'Brussels' and EU climate policies, with political parties questioning these policies based on their perceived economic and social impacts. The threats are real, but so are the economic and social impacts of inaction.

As argued in this book, one of the greatest risks for many countries, particularly in Central Europe, is underestimating the need for transformation. The region is on a trajectory where the slowdown, postponement, or outright undermining of necessary changes and investments poses a significant long-term threat – the risk that short-term, questionable interests may be prioritised at the expense of long-term prospects, potentially missing the opportunity to 'catch the train'. The limits of capitalism in effectively addressing climate change do not mean that creative destruction is not happening.

2.2. Political Priorities

The need for creative destruction, restructuring, and building a new climate-resilient economy is becoming increasingly urgent. As the fastest-warming continent in the world, the European Union faces significant impacts that are either caused or exacerbated by climate change. It starts with the environment: more than 50 % of Europe's ecosystems are threatened by various environmental problems. On average, 700,000 hectares of forest land burn each year, and severe flooding continues to drive up economic costs (EEA, 2024).

According to Giovanni Forzieri's team (Forzieri et al., 2018), climate-related costs for the EU+ were estimated at €3.4 billion per year in 2018. This figure is projected to rise to approximately €9.3 billion (with an uncertainty range of €5.2 to €14.2 billion) after 2020, reaching €19.6 billion (uncertainty range €12.5 to €34.0 billion) by 2050 and €37.0 billion (uncertainty range €21.3 to €53.2 billion) by 2080. Heatwaves are expected to be the dominant factor, accounting for up to 92% of total damages, particularly in sectors like transport, with road damage and railway reconstruction posing major costs. However, investments in infrastructure represent only a fraction of the future expenses required for both climate change mitigation and adaptation.

The rationale behind climate policies is often narrowly perceived as addressing environmental issues. However, these goals are also grounded in strong economic and social foundations. The European Green Deal (EGD) should not be viewed merely as an expense but as an investment. Its declared aim is to tackle climate and environmental challenges by transforming the EU into a modern, secure, resource-efficient, and competitive economy, integrating environmental, economic, and social policies to reduce future impacts and costs.

Political commitments and investments have yielded positive outcomes, as evidenced by the fact that CO_2 emissions in the EU are declining despite continued economic growth – a phenomenon known as decoupling. However, there has been no significant reduction in the EU's ecological footprint, indicating that some emissions are simply outsourced through the importation of products and services from other countries. Combined with the historical emissions debt accrued since the Industrial Revolution, this dynamic shapes the EU's position in global climate negotiations, where it aims to serve as a model of successful transformation.

The transformation the EU is undergoing – and will continue to experience – has deeper roots than environmental concerns alone. Shifting geopolitics and evolving global patterns of production and consumption are driving forces. It is a competition for leadership in green technologies and know-how for restructuring economies based on the principles of ecological modernisation. Countries that take strategic, proactive steps toward climate neutrality may secure substantial competitive advantages. Central Europe still has the opportunity to leverage its political commitments and access to resources, including EU cohesion funds, to catch up with this process.

From a capital perspective, there is a need to balance the interests of both traditional and emerging economies. For new businesses, significant risks are associated with potential slowdowns, postponements, or cuts to green transitions, which affect necessary investments. For traditional industries, especially those reliant on fossil fuels, rapid transformation may spell the end. Considering the growing impacts and costs of global warming, pressure for more effective measures and faster reductions in greenhouse gas emissions will likely increase. While many may hold onto the illusion that the problem will resolve itself, there is no turning back – ignoring the issue will not make it disappear. In this context, both mitigation (emission reductions) and adaptation to climate change face significant risks if actions are delayed. The window for harnessing the potential benefits of early responses is closing quickly.

The costs of early social and economic changes, along with the benefits of rapid transformation, are likely to be lower than those of a slow and delayed reaction. Contrary to the rhetoric of growing anti-environmental populism, Europeans are increasingly facing socio-ecological challenges stemming from a delayed and prolonged transformation (EEA, 2024a). In other words, EU citizens are already bearing the higher costs associated with incomplete transitions to new energy and food systems. Over the past few decades, this has contributed to a dramatic rise in social inequalities, including energy poverty, unequal access to sustainable mobility, food insecurity, and disparities in health outcomes related to air pollution. Ignoring, delaying, or slowing down necessary changes carries both environmental and economic costs.

Resistance to this transformation is understandable. The shift to a green economy can lead to job losses in traditional sectors, industries, and services. Decarbonisation fundamentally alters employment structures, making it crucial to offset these losses through investments in education, training, and workforce mobility. The development of green technologies and renewable resources can create new jobs and promote economic growth, but these sectors will require strong support to thrive.

Here, the welfare state – often critically underdeveloped in Central Europe – can provide a buffer and safety net during the transition. Investments in energy efficiency can reduce energy costs for households and businesses, but they require substantial subsidies. Increasing the share of renewable energy will reduce dependence on fossil fuel imports, enhancing energy security, but this also necessitates a robust, centralised energy policy. In this context, strong state investments and subsidies often clash with the increasingly dominant neoliberal paradigm, which emphasises market-driven solutions over public intervention.

2.3. Mitigation and Outlook

Despite various tendencies, the legally binding political consensus in the European Union is moving towards climate neutrality by 2050, with the goal of gradually but significantly reducing greenhouse gas emissions, particularly carbon dioxide from the burning of fossil fuels. The EU currently contributes around 8 % of global emissions, while playing a significant role in the global effort to mitigate climate change through innovative approaches, such as the Emissions Trading System (ETS). Between 1990 and 2020, emissions in the EU decreased by approximately 24 %, with targets set to reduce emissions by 55 % by 2030 (compared to 1990 levels), achieve a 90 % reduction by 2040, and reach climate neutrality by 2050.

In recent decades, significant progress in reducing carbon dioxide emissions has been made, particularly in the energy sector and in buildings.

Moving towards climate neutrality presents key challenges for energy production and consumption. Europe will need stable and affordable electricity sources for both industry and households. If Central Europe is to maintain its industrial base – partially built on metallurgy and heavy industry – it must create a stable price environment for businesses while supporting the transition to electrification and the adoption of hydrogen technologies. The abrupt disconnection from Russia as an energy supplier has had varying impacts across the EU. The effects were marginal or negligible in Spain and Scandinavia, while energy prices skyrocketed in the Czech Republic and Poland and required heavy subsidies in Slovakia and Hungary.

Central Europe's bet for the future lies in the nuclear industry. In 2021, Poland reaffirmed plans to develop 6–9 GWe of nuclear energy, with the first of six 1–1.5 GWe units planned to be operational by 2033, followed by five more units every 2–3 years. Slovakia, Hungary, and the Czech Republic are investing heavily in the expansion of existing nuclear power plants.

Setting aside the complex debates surrounding the costs and impacts of nuclear energy, the feasible plan involves combining nuclear power with renewable energy sources. When utilising renewables, it is essential to consider the potential for local use, ownership, and management in the medium and long term. Past experiences with supporting these resources should be assessed, particularly to simplify administrative procedures for operators and to set appropriate purchase prices. Measures under the Fit-for-55 package include a review of the EU Emissions Trading System (EU ETS), which currently projects emissions approaching zero as early as 2040. These outlooks could pave the way for long-term changes in the energy and industrial sectors.

The Energy Performance of Buildings Directive (EPBD) defines zero-emission standards for new buildings, sets improved minimum energy performance requirements for non-residential buildings, and focuses more on renovating apartments with the poorest energy performance. It also includes provisions to simplify the energy recovery process. While progress in recent years has been remarkable, implementing further changes will become increasingly costly. Regional disparities in economic performance and investment opportunities will play a critical role in determining progress.

This is an extremely sensitive area from a Central European perspective. Given historical development patterns, population distribution, and demographic trends, many people live in old, energy-inefficient houses, particularly vulnerable groups such as pensioners and residents of economically lagging regions affected by deindustrialisation. The combination of low incomes and high renovation costs will require extensive assistance and subsidies.

Negative trends are also evident in the transport sector. The principle of increasing costs applies here, where each additional percentage reduction in emissions becomes more expensive than the last. It will be crucial to observe how Central Europe copes with this transition, especially as, from 2028, carbon charges under the expanded Emissions Trading System (ETS2) will apply to emissions from road transport fuels, buildings, and small industrial facilities not currently covered by the system.

Unfavourable trends in transport emissions should be addressed through investments in public transport infrastructure, stricter emission standards for new vehicles, and the gradual transition of the automotive industry to electrification. These areas put considerable pressure on public budgets for infrastructure and on individual consumers regarding the costs of new vehicles.

The shift to zero-emission vehicles is expected to accelerate. To promote electrification, the EU has strengthened the Alternative Fuels Infrastructure Regulation (AFIR), aimed at improving coordination and the development of recharging infrastructure. Although this area generates strong political tensions with parts of the industry and consumers, efforts to slow down the transition to new technologies are not aligned with the strategies of key European car manufacturers. In fact, the industry is inclined to accelerate the shift, particularly towards electric vehicles, but requires stronger support from the European Commission and member states.

Agricultural emissions present a more complex challenge, as the EU must balance food security and strategic autonomy with the evolving impacts of climate change on food production. In September 2024, the final report of the Strategic Dialogue on the Future of EU Agriculture, titled Common Prospects for Agriculture and Food in Europe, was published. Its proposals include options for reducing emissions while enhancing strategic autonomy. The COVID-19 pandemic highlighted the strategic importance of food security, and a key area for future action will be the reform of the Common Agricultural Policy (CAP).

Given Central Europe's historical reliance on heavy industry and manufacturing, the future of these sectors remains an open question. Affordable and reliable energy sources are part of the challenge; the other is ensuring fair competition within the EU single market. The gradual phase-out of free emission allowances for industry is linked to the introduction of the Carbon Border Adjustment Mechanism (CBAM), which aims to level the playing field for EU industries competing with non-EU producers not subject to equivalent carbon pricing. This system is still in its early stages and does not yet function optimally, posing significant risks for European producers of steel and other materials.

As an open economy, the EU will be influenced by global changes, such as supply chain shifts and evolving global production and consumption patterns. The key question now is whether it is possible to significantly reduce greenhouse gas emissions while maintaining the EU's competitiveness and social stability – issues that are crucial for the future of Central European countries.

2.4. Adaptation and Outlook

In the context of adverse global trends and climate change scenarios, adaptation is becoming an increasingly dominant focus in the EU's strategic planning. Adaptation encompasses economic, social, political, and environmental dimensions, with early, proactive measures designed to mitigate potential impacts in both the short and long term. In the absence of effective solutions to the core limitations of the global capitalist system, the only viable strategy is to slow down the process through mitigation while doing everything possible to adapt. Although the most pessimistic climate change scenarios may resemble scenes from apocalyptic films, adaptation remains essential.

Being a leader in adaptation is seen by the EU as crucial for business resilience and global competitiveness. A stable business environment reduces risks associated with climate-related disruptions and creates new opportunities for developing innovative materials, products, and services tailored to a changing climate. In its Competitiveness Compass for the EU, the European Commission calls for improved resilience and enhanced preparedness, including strengthening critical infrastructure, integrating climate resilience into urban planning, deploying nature-based solutions, developing nature credits, and promoting adaptation in agriculture while safeguarding food security (EC, 2025).

The EU's adaptation strategies can be broadly divided into external and internal frameworks. Externally, the focus is on maintaining geopolitical influence, providing foreign aid, and securing the Union's borders. Globally, the intensity of climate change impacts varies significantly. In many parts of Africa and Asia, environmental degradation is accelerating, water availability is declining, and agricultural productivity is falling. These conditions are driving displacement and migration from regions that are becoming increasingly uninhabitable and economically unsustainable.

Developed countries, particularly in Europe, are facing – and will continue to face – increasing pressure from climate refugees seeking asylum. This trend is straining member states' social services, already weakened by austerity measures, and contributing to growing political tensions.

Trends in Climate Change-Induced Migration

According to the Intergovernmental Panel on Climate Change (IPCC), one of the most significant impacts of climate change will be the massive global movement of people caused by erosion, drought, coastal flooding, and the collapse of agriculture (IPCC 2007, 2022, 2023). In many parts of Africa, drought and water scarcity are expected to displace millions of people. Similarly, environmental degradation and contamination in the industrial regions of Southeast Asia represent a ticking time bomb with a wide range of potential impacts that can only be roughly predicted today.

The rate of migration is difficult to estimate. A report by the International Federation of the Red Cross (IFRC, 2017) estimates that more than 5,000 people are displaced daily due to climate-related events. The IPCC (2007) also identifies climate change as a major driver of increased migration, predicting that by 2080, 'many millions' of people will be forced to migrate.

The International Organization for Migration (IOM) projects that by 2050, around 200 million people worldwide will have to leave their homes due to environmental changes (UNDESA, 2009). Other studies estimate this number could reach as high as 1.2 billion by 2050 (IEP, 2020). While these figures are uncertain, they represent a dramatic increase in displacement. For comparison, the United Nations High Commissioner for Refugees (UNHCR) reported that 'only' 60 million people were forcibly displaced for political and security reasons in 2014 (UNHCR, 2015).

The 2015 European migrant crisis, marked by a significant increase in the movement of refugees, highlighted the challenges of managing large-scale human displacement. While migration can be suppressed through draconian measures – at the cost of human lives lost at sea – it cannot be completely stopped. Central Europe's response to mass migration was notably extreme. Hungary built fences along its southern border, while Poland erected barriers along its border with Belarus. All four Visegrád countries opposed the EU's migrant redistribution mechanisms, calling instead for hardline solutions. Refugees were often portrayed in local media as economic migrants seeking to exploit the European welfare system.

But is someone whose farm can no longer produce crops due to water scarcity caused by climate change an economic or a climate migrant? Fences and increased military patrols in the Mediterranean Sea cannot stop the inevitable consequences of shifting temperatures and changing precipitation patterns. More and more regions across the globe will gradually become uninhabitable.

The EU – and Central Europe within it – can only slow this trend by providing substantial support and investing heavily in adaptation measures for vulnerable countries. A key outcome of the COP29 climate summit, held in Baku, Azerbaijan, in 2024, was the commitment by developed countries to contribute $300 billion annually by 2035 to support developing nations. However, the global cost of climate change-related damage is projected to reach between $1.7 trillion and $3.1 trillion per year by 2050 (WEF, 2023).

The economic impacts of climate change will also be closely linked to disruptions in global supply chains. The EU relies heavily on developing countries for raw materials, manufacturing, and agricultural products. Climate change can destabilise these supply chains through extreme weather events and crop failures, leading to fluctuations in the availability and prices of goods and commodities. Market volatility will rise, affecting global commodity prices and financial markets. For example, water shortages and declining agricultural yields in Asia could trigger sharp increases in food prices across European markets.

Europe must adapt to shifting geopolitical dynamics, where climate change is likely to act as a trigger or accelerator of regional instabilities and conflicts. It will exacerbate resource scarcity (e.g. water and food), leading to tensions and conflicts in vulnerable regions. Such instability can spill over into neighbouring countries, potentially requiring international interventions and peacekeeping efforts. Competition for resources and the growing demand for humanitarian aid will heighten geopolitical tensions and strain international relations.

Ignoring the global dimension of climate adaptation could result in enormous costs. By addressing root causes and investing in preventive measures in developing countries, the EU can mitigate the indirect effects of climate change on its own societies and economies. However, the longer these investments are delayed, the more expensive they will become as climate impacts intensify.

At the same time, climate adaptation presents opportunities for European businesses to develop and deploy innovative technologies, particularly in agriculture and water management. Providing technical and financial assistance to developing countries for sustainable technologies and climate adaptation should be viewed as a strategic investment, not merely a cost.

The external dimension of adaptation must be complemented by internal measures and investments. Many European countries are already experiencing significant economic losses due to climate change (ECB, 2022). It will be critical to address risks related to extreme weather events, public health, and agricultural productivity. The EU and its member states need to improve risk assessments, strengthen infrastructure resilience, and mitigate the impacts on energy production, water availability, food security, and soil health in both urban and rural areas.

Agriculture will face some of the greatest challenges. Long-term economic trends will be exacerbated by droughts and shifting water cycles. Soil degradation and biodiversity loss are also expected to worsen across Europe. Countries like Poland, with its fragmented agricultural sector, and Hungary, which focuses heavily on large-scale export-oriented farming, will be particularly vulnerable. Farmers may experience declining yields, rising debt, and health issues due to environmental stressors. This could accelerate the concentration of land ownership in Central Europe, favouring extensive, industrial farming practices over small-scale, sustainable agriculture.

In the short term, crop yields in higher latitudes may benefit from a global temperature rise of 1–3°C. However, as temperatures continue to rise, yields will peak and eventually decline. Overall agricultural production is expected to decrease due to more frequent floods, prolonged droughts, and heatwaves. Key crops such as maize, wheat, and other cereals will suffer yield reductions, which will also affect livestock farming. The structure of cultivated crops will need to change, with expanded irrigation systems in drier southern regions and new measures to combat emerging plant diseases.

Extreme weather events will also impose significant costs on infrastructure and public health. Central Europe's transportation and technical infrastructure, much of which is decades old, will be particularly vulnerable. Rising temperatures will put additional pressure on healthcare systems, leading to more cases of heat-related illnesses and exacerbating pre-existing health conditions (EEA, 2024). Public awareness campaigns and preventive health strategies will be essential to mitigate these impacts.

Conservative estimates from the European Environment Agency indicate that the economic losses and human casualties caused by extreme weather events are already severe – and continue to rise. Figure 5 provides data on annual economic losses caused by weather- and climate-related extreme events in EU member states between 1980 and 2022.

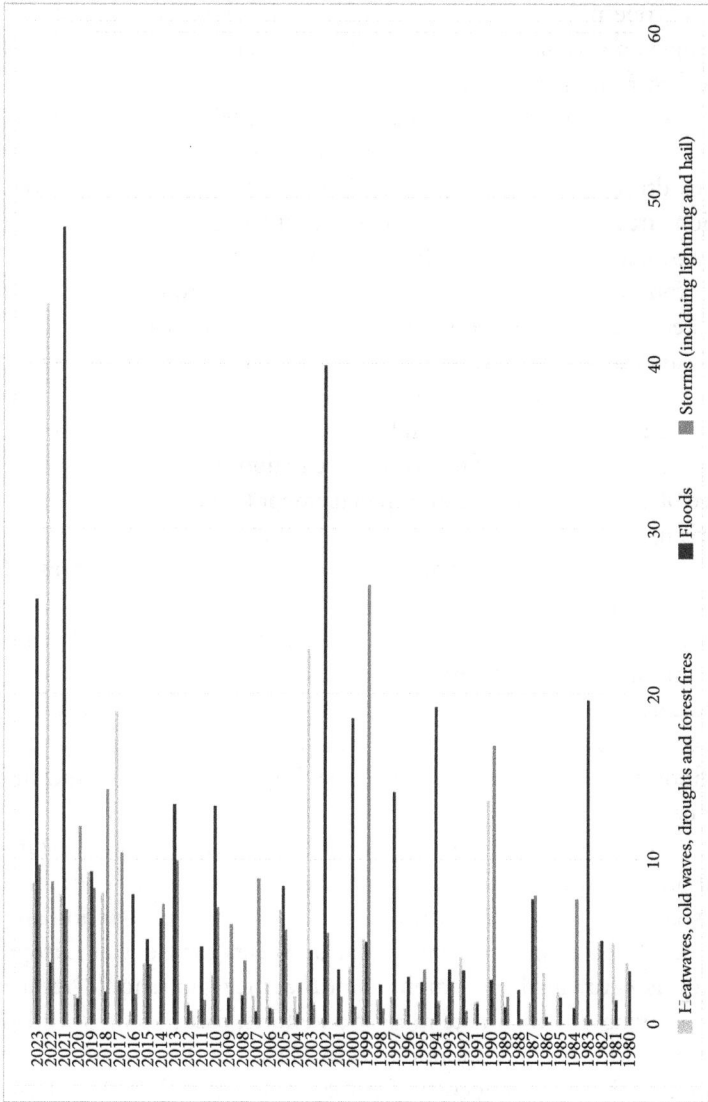

Figure 5: Annual economic losses caused by weather- and climate-related extreme events in EU member states.
Source: EEA, 2024. <https://www.eea.europa.eu/en/analysis/indicators/economic-losses-from-climate-related>

Central Europe must anticipate and address the significant impacts of climate change on various sectors of the economy. The tourism industry is among the first to be severely affected. For instance, the economies of ski resorts at lower altitudes are already becoming unsustainable, with ski lifts remaining profitable only at higher elevations. In Central Europe, this generally means altitudes above 1,200 metres above sea level (m.a.s.l.). However, such locations are relatively scarce, and economic interests often conflict with the need to protect landscapes and biodiversity.

Summer tourism is also facing challenges. Paradoxically, the usability of existing water bodies and the seasonal appeal of mountains and cities may temporarily increase as people seek alternative recreational options. However, long-term trends point to adverse consequences of climate change, including extreme heat, water shortages, and ecosystem degradation, which will undermine the sustainability of tourism in the region. This underscores the importance of effective planning and management to ensure the resilience of the tourism industry.

According to European Commission estimates, every euro invested in anti-flood measures saves an additional six euros in flood-related costs (EC, 2013). Between 1980 and 2022, total climate-related losses in EU member states amounted to €650.5 billion (EEA, 2024). Reports on floods in Europe indicate a gradual increase in their frequency, expanding impacts, and rising costs of mitigation and recovery efforts. At the same time, investments in flood prevention measures are growing but still lag behind the escalating needs.

Central Europe faces a critical dilemma: how to secure these necessary investments in the context of slowing economic growth, demographic decline, emerging security threats, and shifting global patterns of production and consumption. As economic indicators and prospects for Central Europe worsen, there is a growing belief among some that the region should 'return to basics' – slowing down climate mitigation efforts, focusing on selective adaptation, and prioritising economic growth. However, this approach risks underestimating the escalating costs of climate inaction and the long-term benefits of proactive investment in sustainable, climate-resilient measures and practices.

2.5. Climate Change as an Economic Challenge

As early as 2006, a team led by British economist Nicholas Stern estimated, based on formal economic models, that failing to address climate change would result in total costs and risks equivalent to a loss of at least 5% of global GDP annually. This loss would persist indefinitely into a far-reaching and problematic future. According to Stern, if a broader range of risks and impacts were considered, the estimated damage could rise globally to at least 20% of GDP. On the other hand, the cost of action – reducing greenhouse gas emissions to avoid the worst impacts of climate change – would require annual investments equivalent to just 1% of global GDP (Stern, 2006). In other words, we can globally invest 1% today or face the need for 20% of GDP later.

The European Union's ambitious targets, as outlined in the European Green Deal, build on this logic of early action and aim to make the Union climate-neutral by 2050. The EU committed to spending at least 20% of its budget on climate action during the 2014–2020 period, a figure that increased to 30% in the 2021–2027 budget, or approximately €87 billion annually. However, this amount represents less than 10% of the total investment required to achieve the 2030 targets, estimated at around €1 trillion annually, with the remaining funds expected to come from national governments and private sources (ECA, 2023). The challenge is that it remains unclear where these resources will come from, and there is a significant risk of rising national and corporate debt. According to the International Monetary Fund, based on a New Keynesian dynamic general equilibrium model, primary deficits in advanced economies could increase by approximately 0.4 percentage points of GDP over the coming decades due to policy packages designed to achieve net-zero emissions by 2050 (IMF, 2023). Inevitably, part of these expenditures will need to be borne by people and households.

It is not surprising that the cost of action creates reactions. Partly because of the pressure on European and national state budgets, and partly because these costs are becoming subjects of political debate that can influence elections. There are voices in Europe calling for abandoning the entire political framework of climate change policies and focusing on a laissez-faire approach to global economic competition – a model adopted by the US government after the 2024 elections.

For those who, based on scientific data and models, see the environmental, social, and economic costs of climate change as a serious problem, this political shift poses significant challenges. Part of the response lies in attempting to reframe the public debate. Investments in a low-carbon and efficient economy should not only be viewed as costs but also as opportunities to boost productivity, competitiveness, and resource savings.

Authors like Anthony Giddens (2009) argue that the primary motivation for supporting climate policy is not necessarily climate protection itself but rather energy security – though both goals ultimately align. Early estimates suggested that meeting the EU's energy goals would save billions of euros on oil and natural gas imports, create thousands of jobs, and enhance energy security. Furthermore, integrating the European energy market could increase GDP by 0.6 % to 0.8 % (EC, 2009).

The initial investments required present a significant hurdle for the EU. According to the new European Competitiveness Strategy, achieving digitisation, decarbonisation, and increased defence capacity will necessitate sharply raising the investment share in Europe by approximately five percentage points of GDP to levels not seen since the 1960s and 1970s – an unprecedented increase. By comparison, the additional investments provided by the Marshall Plan between 1948 and 1951 amounted to approximately 1–2 % of GDP annually (EK, 2024a). Reducing greenhouse gas emissions and adapting to climate change will have significant economic impacts, requiring careful prioritisation of goals and diversification of funding sources.

Mitigation and adaptation are expensive, as are social services on a continent grappling with demographic decline and increasing defence budget pressures. While at the time of the European Green Deal's adoption, climate change topped the list of priorities, a few years later the rhetoric is shifting. Member states are more aware that ambitious targets come with rising economic and social costs, which will only grow over time. Each additional percentage reduction in emissions will be more complex and expensive than the last. Achieving the EU's 2030, 2040, and 2050 targets will require emission reduction rates to increase by approximately 2.7 times their current pace (EEA, 2024).

This will necessitate radical changes to existing legislative frameworks and funding structures while raising the question of how much economies and people in the EU can bear, especially as key global competitors – like the United States – abandon, at least for the time being, climate investments altogether, and China, despite massive investments, remains cautious about each step toward its 2060 climate neutrality goal.

Central Europe faces two fundamental challenges here: how to capture these diverse economic trends to participate in the transition, and how to adapt to changing conditions. After three decades of neoliberal reforms, research and development are dominantly dependent on EU funding. Foreign direct investment in green technologies can hardly follow previous models that relied heavily on cheap, educated labour. That labour is no longer as cheap, and demographic changes are reducing its availability.

Massive investments will be required for water resource management, agricultural improvements, and increased energy consumption for cooling. What will this mean for the region's economy and social systems? The European economy is deeply embedded in international networks and must remain competitive within them. Member states are already heavily indebted, and few can afford the scale of investments required.

In 2024, the European Central Bank published predictions on the cumulative costs, as a percentage of GDP, associated with addressing key challenges through 2030. The report estimates the annual investment eurozone countries must make from 2024 to 2030 to tackle these challenges. Among the four Central European countries, only Slovakia uses the euro. When comparing Slovakia with the rest of the eurozone, the only favourable parameter is its relatively low debt level, close to 60 % (Figure 6). However, in all other areas, there is significant pressure on the state budget. Particularly concerning is the impact of demographic ageing.

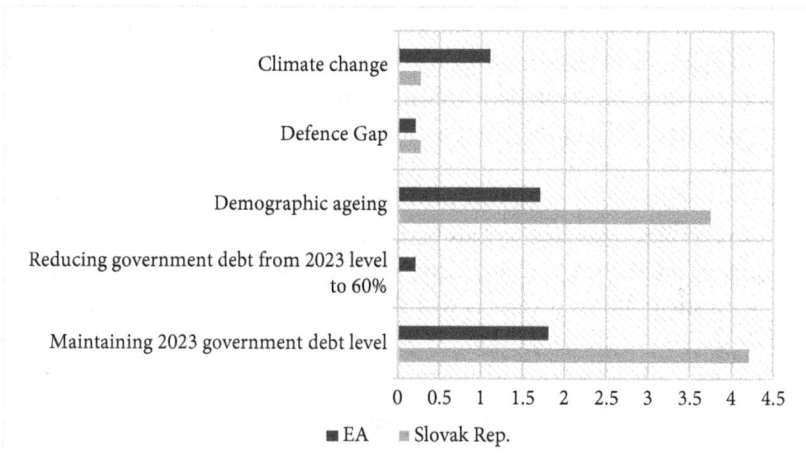

Figure 6: Predictions of cumulative costs in response to specific challenges (as percentages of GDP): Modelling results to 2030.
Source: Adopted from ECB 2024.

Although the models and estimates can be debated – such as comparing the costs of demographic shifts and defence to those of addressing climate change – an important factor for most European countries is the unfavourable combination of high government debt servicing costs and a rapidly deteriorating demographic situation. These factors significantly constrain investment flexibility, making it crucial to integrate the costs of achieving climate neutrality as a cross-cutting priority while seeking synergies across sectors.

Calculations in this area are inherently challenging, and there is no simple answer to how much it will ultimately cost. To some extent, mitigation expenditures can be estimated based on assessments of the energy, transport, agriculture, and building sectors. Adaptation, however, is far more complex. According to European Commission estimates, extreme weather events could, by 2032, increase public debt-to-GDP ratios by more than two percentage points in eight eurozone countries (Gagliardi et al., 2022). The European Central Bank (ECB, 2024) has noted that climate change and the resulting decline in economic activity could disrupt government revenues and lead to higher debt servicing costs. Simulations by the Network of Central Banks and Supervisors for Greening the Financial System (NGFS, 2023) suggest that euro area countries could face significant real output losses.

Reaching the 2040 and 2050 targets will inevitably require serious discussions about tax reforms, the introduction of carbon taxes where they do not yet exist, and the exploration of additional measures to finance a substantial portion of public investments. Moreover, these costs will need to be, at least to some extent, compensated for industries, and current models only partially account for the social costs of the transition and the necessary compensations for low-income groups.

Regardless of which model or estimation is preferred, it is clear that the EU and its member states face serious budgetary consequences stemming from a combination of climate change expenditures and social costs. How global and domestic political pressures will shape the future of climate neutrality goals remains a critical question.

2.6. The New Emerging Framework

Balancing the contradictory interests inherent in the internal logic of capitalism with the rapid and effective reduction of greenhouse gases appears akin to solving the classic 'squaring the circle' problem. The central question revolves around the extent to which profit-driven incentives and the competitive nature of the system can align with the urgent need to reduce carbon emissions and mitigate climate change.

The programme adopted by the European Council for 2024–2029 is based on three pillars: a free and democratic Europe, a strong and secure Europe, and a prosperous and competitive Europe. The priorities are competitiveness and security, with climate change remaining on the agenda but integrated as part of these broader goals rather than treated as a standalone issue. The official formulation of these goals is 'to strengthen competitiveness and become the first climate-neutral continent capable of handling digital and social transformation' (EK, 2024). The emphasis on digital and social transformation reflects emerging challenges, such as artificial intelligence and changing demographics. The European Green Deal's five strategic policy instruments provide a framework focusing on renewable energy promotion, decarbonisation, and the circular economy. However, questions remain regarding the feasibility and sufficiency of the EU's steps toward its 2050 goals.

The emerging framework for the transition to a low-carbon green economy in the EU is increasingly shaped by external and internal pressures to protect the EU economy, increase competitiveness, and enhance security. Decarbonisation is presented by the European Commission as a viable supporting strategy within this broader agenda.

Central Europe finds itself particularly vulnerable in this context, as one of the Union's key steps has been reducing dependence on Russian oil and gas. Historically, the region relied heavily on these supplies through the Friendship Pipelines, built during the era of centrally planned socialism. In the immediate aftermath of the Russia-Ukraine war, energy prices in Central Europe skyrocketed, seriously endangering the region's competitiveness.

While the EU remains committed to its climate goals, there is growing opposition to accelerated transformation among its member states, particularly in Central Europe. This opposition partially reflects uncertainty about global progress, which sends mixed signals. Globally, oil and gas consumption continues to grow. New drilling projects are underway across the Americas, Asia, and the Middle East. Meanwhile, oil- and gas-producing countries have strong economic incentives to increase production and exports, driven by surging demand in China, India, and other nations.

Simultaneously, competition for leadership in green technologies continues to intensify. The European Union is striving to maintain its position in the race to lead global innovation, recognising that this competition is a critical part of the emerging global geopolitical and economic order – a process both shaped and accelerated by climate change. However, China is making enormous progress in AI and IT technologies, while Europe increasingly lags behind.

The transition to a low-carbon economy is a global process and reality. With exceptions like the post-2024 policy shifts in the United States and some political movements in Europe, most countries in both the Global North and South acknowledge the need to address ongoing climate change. Many nations view the transition as an opportunity for economic progress and a leap forward through the rapid development and deployment of green technologies. For instance, it is easier to install solar panels than to build a coal-burning power plant, and electric vehicles are becoming increasingly more accessible than traditional combustion engines. The question remains: who will produce and supply these technologies and products? Here, the prospects for the EU are less optimistic.

Whether countries achieve their declared climate neutrality goals will depend on various socio-economic factors. The logic of the EU approach is based on the premise that those who lag behind risk compromising their competitiveness, security, and social stability. Conversely, those who invest in the transition early will gain a head start while avoiding significantly higher future costs. The speed and management of this transformation will either positively or negatively influence GDP growth. Countries failing to adapt will face a dangerous spiral, as lower growth leads to higher debt servicing costs and fewer resources for necessary investments.

Adaptation, in this logic, should not be viewed merely as an expenditure but as a preventive measure against future losses. The economic consequences of climate change and delayed action may include productivity losses in the EU, supply chain disruptions, and decreased food production. Extreme weather events, particularly water scarcity, will necessitate agricultural adaptation where possible. In regions where adaptation is unfeasible, economic decline, social conflicts, and migration may follow. The European Union has had – and still has – ambitions to provide an example of development patterns where climate neutrality merges with adaptation, economic growth, and well-being for the people. However, whether this vision can succeed in the face of global capitalist dynamics is a question explored in other parts of this book.

Under external and internal pressures, mixed global signals, and growing domestic opposition, the emerging EU framework attempts to reposition climate change as an issue to be addressed within three dimensions: competitiveness, security, and fairness. As the EU increasingly lags behind its primary competitors, particularly in competitiveness, rapid and fundamental changes will be required (EC, 2024). Transforming energy and industry will necessitate substantial investments in new infrastructure and technologies. The short-term economic costs will be high, creating challenges for state budgets and private sector stakeholders. The transition from fossil fuels to renewable energy sources is essential but costly and technically demanding. Changes in transport, housing, and consumption patterns will also reshape industries, requiring European companies to stay competitive with global leaders.

The EU's 'selling point' for climate neutrality and green transformation is increasingly based on the premise that, alongside significant challenges, the process offers opportunities to achieve economic and social sustainability. A successful transition will require swift and coordinated efforts from governments, businesses, civil society, and international partners, but it remains feasible. The underlying logic suggests that these efforts will ultimately pay off if the challenges are effectively addressed, enabling the EU to achieve a greener, more prosperous future for all its citizens.

However, how compatible this optimistic perspective is with the increasingly diverse geopolitical interests and the inherent logic of capitalism remains an open question. A telling sign of changing times is that, while the West once criticised and sought to dismantle protectionist measures abroad, it is now the West that is increasingly attempting to build economic and political fences. A prime example of this shift is the concept of strategic autonomy, which reflects the EU's efforts to reduce dependence on external actors and protect its economic and political interests in an increasingly fragmented global landscape.

2.7. Central European Implications

Central Europe faces numerous external and internal challenges linked to decarbonisation. Externally, these include the shifting landscape of the global economy, the EU's overall competitiveness, the region's position in global production chains, and tensions among member states regarding cohesion policies. Internally, the region grapples with a demographic crisis, the limitations of an economic model reliant on cheap labour, growing regional disparities, and uneven development that fosters inequalities and political divisions between prosperous capitals like Prague and Budapest and declining small towns on the periphery.

Heavy industries and manufacturing, particularly automotive, remain critical sources of well-paid jobs and income in Central Europe. The automotive industry, once the flagship of European industrial excellence, now faces threats from emerging global competitors. Rising energy costs are adversely affecting not only large corporations but also the supplier networks of small and medium-sized enterprises. In this context, decarbonisation represents perhaps the most significant social challenge these countries must address.

It is essential to build a consensus on whether to keep strategic industries, such as iron mills and metal processing, within the EU. In 2024, the US government blocked the sale of US Steel Company to new Japanese owners, citing security concerns. Part of US Steel's assets include a factory in Košice, Slovakia. The production of iron and other strategic materials often falls outside the direct control of the EU or individual member states. However, it will likely be the EU or its member states that will need to subsidise the costly decarbonisation of such industries.

Europe, including the countries in question, lacks a robust green industrial policy. Such a policy should address how to manage inevitable labour market changes associated with digitalisation and decarbonisation while identifying strategies to stimulate and create new job opportunities in sectors tied to the green transition. Decarbonisation will inevitably lead to a decline in employment in polluting sectors ('brown jobs').

However, the optimistic forecasts of increased 'green jobs' that preserve or restore environmental quality are materialising at a slow pace. Countries within this region are competing with one another. According to Bloomberg analyses (BNEF 2024), while Germany attracted $90.32 billion in 2023 and neighbouring Poland secured $14.17 billion in foreign direct investments into the green technologies market, Slovakia managed to draw in only $0.13 billion.

Three potential pathways for the region's approach to decarbonisation can be envisioned. A passive approach involves setting minimal goals and fulfilling EU obligations mechanically without strategic initiatives. A subversive approach would rely on delays, obstruct necessary political and legislative actions, block EU decision-making, and undermine the implementation of already adopted measures. The active scenario involves taking a proactive role in shaping and co-creating changes, focusing on the rapid transformation of the economy while effectively utilising EU financial instruments. Given the analysis of global and European trends, the active scenario is the most viable path forward. It requires shifting from being a passive recipient of change to an active agent of transformation, emphasising strategic planning, investment, and implementation.

The first step in the active scenario is strategic planning and green industrial policy. Central Europe must strengthen strategic planning and develop supportive infrastructure for transitioning to a green economy. Effective use of European Structural and Investment Funds, the Recovery Plan, the Modernisation Fund, and other EU resources – which are temporary – requires clear strategies. After 2027, with a new EU multiannual financial framework, a decrease in EU transfers is anticipated.

Failing to act decisively – through political hesitancy or resistance to change – will weaken Central Europe's competitiveness, increase adaptation and mitigation costs, and squander opportunities to leverage EU cohesion policies. The greatest risk lies in underestimating the transformation's urgency and falling behind.

Climate neutrality must be embedded as a cross-cutting development goal in national strategies, with an emphasis on implementing the measures taken. Central European countries, with their industrial bases heavily reliant on the automotive, heavy, and metallurgical industries, need a vision for these sectors. They must find consensus with the EU and the Single European Market on future green industrial policies. These policies should define priorities for attracting investments, fostering green industries, and transitioning to a low-carbon economy.

Financing is a cornerstone of the green transformation. It requires a strategic combination of public resources, EU funds, and private investments while dismantling subsidies for fossil fuels. Here, the neoliberal policies so far dominantly followed by Central European governments will clash with the need for strategic approaches and instruments such as planning, tax reforms, and new forms of social policies.

Tax reforms can play a critical role. Excise taxes on electricity, gas, and coal, often in the form of implicit carbon taxes, need reform to address inefficiencies and eliminate excessive tax exemptions. A comprehensive review of the tax system, combining progressive taxation with eco-social reforms, is necessary to maintain social cohesion during the green transition. This is particularly challenging given that Central Europe's competitive advantage is largely based on low taxes.

A green industrial policy must address the transition in traditional industries, particularly heavy manufacturing and automotive sectors, aligning them with the principles of the circular economy. Strategic autonomy can support the domestic industrial base, with mechanisms like the Carbon Border Adjustment Mechanism (CBAM) shielding Central Europe from unfair competition in carbon-intensive products such as steel and cement.

The labour market will undergo substantial changes. The decline in 'brown jobs' must be matched with the creation of green jobs and reskilling programmes. European investments in research and innovation are crucial to fostering sustainable economic growth, transformative technologies, and green jobs. However, these investments remain below their potential, and Central European countries are often at the bottom of European comparisons in the number of patents, utilisation of research grants, or added value from the transfer of research to practice.

Large regional disparities across Central Europe will significantly shape the decarbonisation process. Targeted regional decarbonisation strategies involving local governments, regions, and cities are essential. Lessons can be drawn from successful transformations, such as those in former coal mining regions of the Czech Republic and Slovakia.

Social vulnerabilities and poverty pose serious challenges. Many households already feel the burden of transformation, and costs will continue to rise. The newly developed European Social Climate Fund can help, but comprehensive compensation systems combining EU and domestic resources are needed to ensure a just transition without social upheaval.

Broader strategic considerations need to be combined with short-term priorities and ongoing processes that have already begun or are in progress. ETS2 (Emissions Trading System for transport and buildings) will take effect in 2028 (The implementation was postponed due to the resistance of some MS). Central Europe must prepare for these changes by supporting building renovations and advancing public transport infrastructure adapted to climate change.

The upcoming negotiation of the Effort Sharing Budget and LULUCF (Land Use, Land-Use Change, and Forestry) allocations for 2026–2030 and beyond will be critical for climate neutrality plans. The Carbon Removal Certification Framework will open new opportunities for agriculture, especially in Poland and Hungary, to benefit from carbon sequestration initiatives. This requires clear targets, supportive infrastructure, and monitoring systems.

Without swift and strategic action, Central Europe risks falling further behind its core neighbours, missing out on the economic opportunities presented by the green transition, and facing greater challenges in meeting EU climate and sustainability goals. This could lead to long-term economic repercussions, including reduced competitiveness, lower job creation in emerging sectors, and increased reliance on traditional, carbon-intensive industries that may become obsolete in the coming decades.

The intertwined logics of global geopolitics, economic accumulation, and capital growth create structural barriers to the radical changes needed for long-term climate action. Yet this should not prevent us from doing what is possible and feasible in the short run. While systemic limits pose challenges, they should not lead to passivity. Testing the boundaries of the system and pushing for reforms remain essential steps toward mitigating climate change and achieving climate neutrality. Central Europe's ability to successfully navigate the challenges of decarbonisation depends on adopting an active, forward-looking approach that combines strategic planning, robust financing, regional equity, and innovative policies. While the limits of capitalism may constrain the transformation, seizing available opportunities and leveraging existing resources are critical.

Between Geopolitics, Capitalism and Climate Change

Central Europe in the twenty-first century faces a complex convergence of crises that intertwine geopolitics, capitalism, neoliberalism's self-destructive tendencies, and climate change. These forces do not operate in isolation; rather, they shape and are shaped by one another, producing a dynamic landscape where economic interests, political power, and environmental challenges intersect. In this chapter, we take a closer look at the most significant of these forces.

The system of production and consumption, originally invented in the West, has achieved global dominance. Climate change has become a geopolitical catalyst, influencing not only migration patterns but also resource conflicts and the balance of power between nations. The global response to climate change reveals deep-seated inequalities within the world system, exacerbating polarisation and competition among nations and blocs, which undermines any potential for a stronger global climate agreement.

Metabolic rift, the treadmill of production, and stimulated consumption are now global phenomena. A persistent problem in the debate about the green transformation is the focus on addressing symptoms rather than root causes. Energy production and transport are often highlighted, but there is little debate about why our consumption remains drastically high and continues to grow. While we discuss ecological design and new technologies, even if all cars were powered by electricity, this would not solve the complex issues surrounding the production and disposal of these vehicles, nor would it address increasing traffic and pollution in a world with a growing population and rising purchasing power. It is unsurprising that the solutions gaining the most traction are those that do not threaten the vested interests of powerful business groups (e.g. carbon substitution) or those that present lucrative business opportunities (e.g. carbon capture and storage, or emissions trading).

The engine of growth is the need for capital to invest and expand, primarily through consumption. This consumption is more of a social construct than a necessity, and it must be stimulated by various marketing strategies. Consumption is sold to us as a measure of quality of life and personal satisfaction. Taken to the extreme, any appeal to reduce consumption can be perceived as an attack on the essence of the system – and, at its core, on individual freedom. In the logic of capitalism, the growing number of problems is paradoxically seen as positive, as it stimulates investment and, therefore, generates profit. Natural resources are treated as replaceable income when, in fact, they should be treated as capital because they are finite and will eventually be depleted (Schumacher, 1973).

It is in this context that we globally and regionally discuss the green transformation. When viewed through the lens of creative destruction – a concept originally coined by Joseph Schumpeter – we see that the timing for this transformation is far from ideal. As the future of industry in Central Europe hangs in the balance, the neoliberal state's diminished capacity to guide economic and social transitions poses significant risks. How decarbonisation efforts unfold within a political and economic framework that prioritises deregulation, market freedom, and minimal state intervention will be crucial. These conditions raise serious questions about the viability of achieving a just and sustainable green transition – one that risks trapping many people in cycles of low-paid, insecure work. This transformation demands deep structural changes that simultaneously address the green transition, shifting demographics, labour market challenges, and rising inequalities – all while the neoliberal state replaces the welfare state.

The prevailing approach is based on the belief that every problem can be addressed through managerial and technical solutions. The theory of environmental modernisation, which dominates mainstream debate today, builds on this assumption. According to Kilbourne and Carlson (2008:5), the fixation on technical solutions is also present in well-intentioned environmental education efforts. These often focus on specific problems, such as air pollution, waste reduction, or energy conservation, but fail to address the core issues embedded in our economic and social systems.

Just a few years ago, we at least rhetorically engaged in discussions about sustainable development – a concept with varying meanings but one that attempted to integrate economic, social, and environmental dimensions of progress. Today, the discourse has shifted. At best, we speak of ecological modernisation, but increasingly, the conversation is dominated by the pursuit of 'competitiveness'. However, competition on a dying planet may ultimately mean fighting for basic resources like water and food.

3.1. Global Inequalities and the World System

Ulrich Beck, in his influential work *Risk Society: Towards a New Modernity* (1992), argues that certain modern risks, particularly environmental ones like smog, are democratic in the sense that they transcend traditional social boundaries such as class, nationality, or income. However, he also acknowledges that the distribution of these risks is not entirely equal. In practice, poorer and marginalised communities often bear the brunt of environmental hazards. When we apply this framework to climate change, it becomes clear that while the crisis is global, its effects are unevenly distributed. Some regions and countries are exposed earlier and more severely, while others may believe they have more time to adapt – or at least act as if they do.

Geographically, the impact of climate change is already, and will increasingly be, distributed unequally. A country's location, political situation, and economic and social strength influence its ability to adapt and shape the distribution of risks within its borders. While many of the most devastating impacts are already unfolding in the Global South, the wealth and resources needed for adaptation are overwhelmingly concentrated in the Global North. This creates a double burden of marginalisation for those living in the most affected areas who also lack the means to adapt. As the number of people facing this double marginalisation grows, the result is often political instability, conflict, and migration.

Climate change is, therefore, a perfect example of a global political dilemma. It raises sensitive questions about why some countries are poor and who has benefitted – and who has not – from the economic trends of the last few centuries. It continues the discourse on post-colonialism, opens discussions about resource sharing, examines the effects of industrial development, and touches on long-standing debates within development theory.

On one hand, the sources of greenhouse gas emissions are historically rooted in industrialised nations. The origins of CO_2 emissions trace back to the Industrial Revolution, and the world is now grappling with the accumulated impacts of centuries of fossil fuel combustion. On the other hand, the most severe effects of climate change are being felt in developing countries (Stern 2006; UNEP 2007; IPCC 2007, 2011).

This division is reflected in national priorities and perspectives. Fatu Lefale (2008) categorises countries based on how they perceive and prioritise climate change. The prevailing view in the Global North frames climate change as an environmental-ecological issue, rooted in the belief that it results from humanity's poor stewardship of nature. This perspective positions industrialised nations as victims of environmental degradation, with solutions focused on regulations, market incentives, and ecological modernisation.

In contrast, many countries in the Global South perceive climate change primarily as a human problem, not just an environmental one. They focus on the issue of quality of life and the disproportionate impacts on their populations (Lefale 2008: 15). These differing starting points shape national positions in international negotiations over who should contribute to solving the problem, how much they should contribute, and through what mechanisms. The North emphasises its relationship with nature, seeking to address emissions through technical solutions, market instruments, and ecological modernisation. The South, however, emphasises the right to develop and demands that the North take responsibility for a climate crisis generated by its historical and ongoing patterns of production and consumption. Developing countries argue that wealthy nations must invest in adaptation measures for the people most affected.

The attitude of many developing nations toward the political resolution of climate change can be illustrated by the words of former Malaysian Prime Minister Mahathir Mohamad (1990), who stated: '*The poor do not ask for charity. While the rich cut down their own forests, build their factories spewing poisons, and roam the world in search of cheap resources, the poor remain silent. They are basically paying for the development of the rich. Now the rich claim that they have the right to regulate the development of poor countries, and at the same time, any demand that the rich countries adequately compensate the poor is considered excessive. We were abused as colonies; now we are to be abused again.*'

Climate change, therefore, is much more than a technical problem to be solved through negotiations. It reaches into the roots of global history and reflects the present distribution of benefits and harms. This dynamic aligns with Immanuel Wallerstein's (2000) *world-systems theory*, which describes the global social system as one with defined boundaries, structures, members, rules, and coherence. This system functions through conflicting forces that simultaneously hold it together and pull it apart, as each group seeks to maximise its own advantage. The world system operates like an organism, remaining stable in some respects while rapidly changing in others.

A key characteristic of the world system is the power hierarchy between countries in the core, semi-periphery, and periphery. This hierarchy is the result of the expansive development of European economies since the fifteenth century, which gave rise to colonialism and created lasting dependencies. These dependencies persist in modified forms today. Core countries dominate and exploit weaker, poorer societies. Technology – in the broadest sense – is a key determinant of a country's position within this hierarchy. Technological advancements shift over time, moving from dominance in the spice trade and cloth production to control over sectors like investment banking, nanotechnology, and, increasingly, artificial intelligence. While the geographical centres of power have shifted – from the Republic of Venice to the Dutch Provinces, to Great Britain, to the United States, and possibly now to Southeast Asia and China – the fundamental principle of extracting surplus value from the periphery remains unchanged. This process underlies the accumulation of capital.

As Barbosa (2009) points out, global environmental problems must be understood within the context of world-system dynamics. Everything becomes subject to rationalisation and commodification. Rationalisation replaces traditional social relations and ways of life with bureaucratic structures and a homogenised culture – namely, consumerism. Commodification transforms everything into a commodity that can be traded, from natural resources to pollution rights and emissions credits.

Global incqualities among countries in the core, semi-periphery, and periphery are reflected in patterns of environmental degradation. Semi-peripheral and peripheral countries serve as sources of raw materials and dumping grounds for waste from problematic technologies. These are the regions where manufacturing is concentrated, heavily reliant on fossil fuels. Meanwhile, modernisation theory promotes the idea that these countries can 'catch up' through political and economic reforms. Even if countries like China succeed in this race, the overall global inequalities and disparities persist – and continue to grow. In other words, inequality is not disappearing; it is merely shifting.

For Central European countries, this presents a significant dilemma. As previously discussed, the region, long positioned as Europe's semi-periphery, has aspired to join the European core. Recent moves, such as Hungary's increasing alignment with Chinese investments, may signal shifting priorities at the semi-periphery. Simultaneously, Poland is focusing on enhancing ties with the United States. This scenario recalls Antonio Gramsci's (1971) famous observation: *'The crisis consists precisely in the fact that the old is dying and the new cannot be born; in this interregnum, a great variety of morbid symptoms appear.'*

World-systems theory highlights the expansionist economic model developed in the West and globally adopted under capitalism – a model fundamentally incompatible with resolving the climate crisis. Immanuel Wallerstein (2005: 324) poses three essential questions about future development within this system. First, is it possible for every part of the world to achieve the living standards and cultural-institutional frameworks of countries like Denmark? If not, the second question follows: Can the current polarised and socially stratified world survive as we know it? The third question, arising from the second, is: What alternatives does this open up in the context of advancing climate change?

Based on analyses of GDP growth, comparative advantages, and development trajectories, Wallerstein concludes that it is impossible – and contrary to the very principles of the global world system – for every country to achieve the living standards of the most developed nations. While some countries may rise on the global ladder, others will inevitably fall, and the principle of inequality will remain intact.

The world is, on average, economically better off than it was a few decades ago. However, inequalities persist in new forms, and core countries continue to shift. While global wealth increases, the environmental costs multiply, running up against the planet's finite resources.

3.2. The Climate and Geopolitical Stakes

The 1990s, following the collapse of the Soviet Union and the end of the Eastern Bloc, were marked by a wave of hope and optimism, accompanied by expectations of a new global order. The United States emerged as the sole global superpower, and it seemed the world was entering a new era of geopolitics. Perhaps not coincidentally, this period also witnessed significant progress in global climate policies.

The Intergovernmental Panel on Climate Change (IPCC), established by the UN in 1988, began producing increasingly urgent evidence of human influence on the climate and the catastrophic scenarios that could result from unchecked climate change. Data on ecosystem changes, species extinction, shifts in rainfall and temperature patterns, and irreversible environmental impacts accumulated rapidly. It also became increasingly clear that these environmental changes would have far-reaching economic and social repercussions, including disruptions to agriculture, the spread of diseases (such as malaria moving to higher latitudes), mass migration, and conflicts over scarce resources like water and arable land.

In response to this growing scientific consensus, the UN Framework Convention on Climate Change (UNFCCC) was established during the 1992 Earth Summit in Rio de Janeiro. The convention's primary objective was to stabilise greenhouse gas concentrations in the atmosphere at levels that would prevent dangerous interference with the climate system. Despite criticisms of its vagueness, the convention laid the groundwork for the Kyoto Protocol, which committed industrialised countries to reducing their emissions by specific percentages. However, even these relatively modest reductions – 5.7–8% below 1990 levels by 2012 – provoked defensive reactions from industries and governments. Russia ratified the protocol only in 2004, while the United States, the world's largest CO_2 emitter at the time, signed the treaty but never ratified it.

If the Kyoto Protocol was criticised for being too weak, its successor – the Paris Agreement – marked a shift toward even more flexible commitments. Instead of binding reduction targets, countries now determine their own nationally determined contributions (NDCs) to meet the treaty's aims. However, these contributions lack a strong international enforcement mechanism, making accountability difficult and progress inconsistent.

Is the global effort to address climate change an example of failure? The answer is both yes and no. The preparation and implementation of environmental policies is a complex process, whether at the national level or within entities like the European Union. The mere continuation of international negotiations represents progress, yet the broader economic and social context of climate change mitigation and adaptation suggests that the path to any meaningful global agreement will be extremely arduous and complicated – raising the pressing question of whether we have enough time.

Global efforts to combat climate change have yet to resolve the fundamental dilemma between the right to development and the limits of growth. Paradoxically, some policies have even facilitated the further export of environmental problems. To ease resistance from developing countries regarding emissions reductions, the UN introduced the principle of 'common but differentiated responsibilities'. This approach acknowledged that many countries had historically contributed little to greenhouse gas emissions and reaped minimal benefits from industrialisation yet were being asked to bear the same costs as those nations most responsible for climate change. However, this 'right to emissions' often results in increased pressure on the climate, while the economic profits generated frequently end up outside the borders of the countries asserting this right, aiding emission reduction efforts in wealthier nations instead.

The absence of stronger international conventions has led to the phenomenon of carbon leakage, where production shifts to countries with weaker environmental regulations. This means that carbon dioxide emissions rise in one country as a consequence of emission reduction policies implemented elsewhere. As industries move to countries with lower environmental standards to avoid stricter regulations and higher production costs, global emissions do not decrease but are merely relocated geographically. Carbon leakage is increasingly cited by policymakers in developed countries, including within the EU, as a justification for deregulating and reassessing climate policies, arguing that stringent measures undermine national economies and competitiveness in the global market.

The declared goal of global climate policy is to limit warming to below 2°C – a threshold considered manageable in terms of environmental impacts. Achieving this goal requires climate neutrality in key global blocs, including the EU, China, and the United States, as well as significant commitments from developing countries. However, while developed nations face rising opposition to further commitments, developing countries argue that these demands infringe upon their right to economic growth.

A paradox persists in all agreements to date: even if initial targets were met, they would not be sufficient to halt global warming. More radical measures continue to be postponed, and the longer action is delayed, the higher and more costly the necessary restrictions will become over a shorter timeframe. While the exact extent and scale of climate change impacts remain subjects of debate, there is broad consensus that human activity is the primary driver. Acting sooner rather than later is critical to avoid the compounded effects of inaction.

Yet this 'inaction' must be analysed within the context of a shifting global political landscape. Part of the reason for the shift toward increasingly vague international frameworks lies in the evolving geopolitical dynamics of the twenty-first century. Compared to the 1990s, we now live in a multipolar world dominated by three superpowers: the United States, China, and Russia. These nations – and, in their shadow, many others – perceive binding climate agreements as threats to their national security and economic interests.

John Mearsheimer, in his influential book *The Tragedy of Great Power Politics* (2014), highlights how the logic of great power rivalry profoundly shapes global developments. Mearsheimer's theory of offensive realism rests on several key principles: the anarchy of the international system, the offensive military capabilities of great powers, and the primary goal of states – survival. States, acting as rational actors, strategically pursue survival by accumulating power, which inevitably leads to competition and conflict.

Today, the economic power of states remains deeply tied to fossil fuel-based economies. While small, wealthy nations like Norway can afford ambitious goals such as achieving climate neutrality by 2030, for superpowers, any disruption to their fossil fuel-dependent economic foundations is viewed as a direct threat to national security. This sense of vulnerability is increasingly tied to doctrines like mutually assured destruction (MAD), which posits that the full-scale use of nuclear weapons by any two adversaries would result in total annihilation. While MAD focuses on military conflict, the logic of mutual vulnerability now extends to economic and environmental domains as well.

Global climate targets require global agreements, but rising geopolitical tensions make such deals increasingly elusive. Capitalism, driven by its need for continuous investment and growth, offers opportunities in green technologies and decarbonisation. Yet the contradictions inherent in the very foundations of the global order may, at any time, lead to its collapse – whether in the short term through nuclear conflict or, in the long term, through the unchecked progression of climate change.

The world system is transforming; centres of economic power are shifting geographically, but the fundamental principle of extracting surplus value from the periphery remains unchanged. China's land acquisitions in Africa for agricultural production mirror the historical exploitation of the periphery by European colonial powers. From the perspective of climate change, it doesn't matter whether a ton of carbon dioxide is emitted in the EU or in a developing country. But it does matter who pays for the emissions and who benefits from them.

Cost-benefit debates over climate action collide with intensifying international rivalries and the age-old question of whether capitalism inevitably leads to war. This debate has its roots in Marxist theory. Karl Marx and Friedrich Engels argued that capitalism's inherent drive for profit and competition fosters conditions ripe for conflict. Economic inequalities within and between nations fuel competition for resources, markets, and influence, escalating tensions that can lead to war. The theory of imperialism extends this argument, suggesting that capitalist nations are compelled to colonise and dominate others in pursuit of new markets and resources.

While Mearsheimer's realist perspective acknowledges the role of economic factors in conflicts, it emphasises the central role of anarchy in the international system. In contrast, Norman Angell argued in *The Great Illusion* (1909) that economic interdependence made war irrational, as the costs would outweigh any potential benefits. However, history – particularly the two world wars – has demonstrated that wars are rarely driven solely by cost-benefit analyses.

For decades, the idea that free trade and economic interdependence could reduce the likelihood of conflict – often referred to as the 'capitalist peace' theory – gained traction. However, the Russia-Ukraine war (2022) and escalating tensions in the Middle East (2023) highlight the unresolved structural problems underpinning global power relations among capitalist economies.

The interplay between capitalism's internal logic and the imperative of survival raises pressing questions about the future of global, regional, and national decarbonisation strategies. In the United States, the military-industrial complex – a dominant economic force since Dwight Eisenhower's presidency – continues to shape policy decisions. In the European Union, the growing influence of defence spending adds to fragmentation, as decisions are rooted in the varying interests of member states. Faced with these challenges, the EU must decide where to invest for the future. As economic growth and security increasingly take precedence, decarbonisation and climate neutrality risk being deprioritised. In the shifting global order and the declining relative power of the West, climate may become the first casualty.

3.3. Marx, Metabolic Rift, Infrastructure and Climate Change

The relationship between humans and their environment underwent radical changes during industrialisation and urbanisation – changes that continue to shape our attitudes and priorities today. Karl Marx, one of the earliest and most influential analysts of industrial society's impact on the social sphere, described this dynamic using the concept of the *Metabolic Rift*.

The *Metabolic Rift* focuses on understanding and explaining the evolving relationship between humans and nature through the lens of increasing distance. While Marx's reasoning is rooted in the paradigm of industrialisation and is strongly Eurocentric, his insights into industrialised societies remain thought-provoking. As Barbosa (2009) notes, Marx emphasised humanity's unique ability to think critically and transform its environment. Although some of his claims – such as the idea that natural resources are freely provided by nature and only human labour gives them value – may seem controversial today, his analysis of the growing alienation from nature remains relevant.

Marx argued that the expansion of the capitalist mode of production leads to a weakening of the bond between humans and the natural world, from which they derive their basic resources. This alienation, accelerated by the Industrial Revolution, is at the heart of the *Metabolic Rift*.

As Clark and Foster (2001) note, Marx's concept is not primarily concerned with environmental devastation as we understand it today. At the time, the capacity of nature to absorb waste and industrial emissions seemed limitless, and environmental degradation was not widely discussed. Rather, Marx highlighted how capitalism, in transforming the social sphere, also reshapes humanity's relationship with nature.

The weaker the bond between humans and nature becomes, the more abstract environmental problems appear, making it increasingly difficult to generate consensus around the need for environmental protection. Furthermore, as people's survival depends more on the infrastructure they help create and on spatially distributed patterns of production and consumption, they are less likely to perceive or prioritise the negative impacts associated with these activities.

For example, consider the case of heating with locally sourced wood. Individuals who gather wood from nearby forests directly experience and understand the limits of natural resources. However, when they switch to heating with coal purchased using wages, their relationship with nature changes substantially. They lose direct contact with nature and become distanced from the environmental impacts of coal mining, processing, and transportation. Consequently, their dependence on coal may reduce their concern for the environmental consequences of its production – especially when the environmental damage occurs thousands of kilometres away.

This is not merely a historical phenomenon but remains a significant contemporary issue. A 2010 report by the European Environmental Agency highlights the growing risk of declining public awareness of ecological problems. The report notes that as more people live in large urban settlements with little direct experience of the natural environment, this trend is most pronounced among younger generations (EEA, 2010).

In many developed countries, environmental quality has objectively improved across several parameters, largely due to better regulation and ecological modernisation. However, this improvement is also attributable to the outsourcing of environmentally damaging activities to other regions, particularly developing countries. For instance, environmental degradation in China may not provoke the same public concern as a visible factory chimney polluting the air in one's immediate surroundings. Yet, the outsourcing of production abroad – often framed as a result of stricter environmental standards at home – can influence public opinion when presented as a cause of job losses.

Climate change, with its globalised dimensions and severe local economic and social consequences, often fails to mobilise public action as effectively as local environmental concerns. It is far easier to rally support to stop the dumping of toxic waste in the Venetian Lagoon in Italy than to spark outrage over environmental destruction in Vietnam caused by burning coal to produce goods for export to developed countries. Although the impacts of climate change are increasingly visible in floods, droughts, and forest fires across Europe, the problem is compounded by our dependence on infrastructure built on fossil fuels, providing us with heat, transport, and prosperity.

What the *Metabolic Rift* teaches us is that environmental problems can easily become abstract or deprioritised in the face of other concerns. The alienation of humans from nature may progress further as people living within complex technological infrastructures become increasingly dependent on these systems and support their preservation and expansion – even at the cost of worsening climate impacts. This dependence extends beyond physical survival, such as access to energy, heat, or food, and includes social risks. Threats to infrastructure endanger employment and the broader systems that underpin societal stability.

As individuals become more detached from the natural environment, their understanding of its limits and their willingness to address its degradation diminish. Simultaneously, their reliance on industrial and technological systems reinforces a cycle of dependence, making the pursuit of sustainable solutions increasingly difficult. This dynamic underscores the challenges of addressing climate issues within industrialised societies and highlights the need for systemic change in the relationship between humans, nature, and the structures of production and consumption. Easier said than done in a system that has growth and expansion at its core.

3.4. Treadmill and the Brave New World of Stimulated Consumption

Besides the growing alienation from nature, since the second half of the twentieth century, there have been drastic changes in production and consumption patterns, which are crucial for understanding the deeper causes and limitations of climate change policies and measures. The economic model of capitalism, as developed in the industrialised countries of the North and now globally dominant, depends on perpetual growth.

In 1980, Allan Schnaiberg published his groundbreaking work *The Environment: From Surplus to Scarcity*. According to Schnaiberg (1980), environmental problems in modern society have four main causes: population growth, technological changes, a boom in consumption, and a boom in production. He identifies the degradation of the environment in the twentieth century as a result of both qualitative and quantitative changes in production. Machines have replaced human labour, which has, on one hand, led to job losses and, on the other hand, increased the consumption of energy and natural resources. The growing number of products and services requires buyers. The second part of the problem thus lies in socially constructed consumption, created by producers. Schnaiberg's work led to the formulation of the *Treadmill Theory*, which was further developed by Kenneth Gould and David Pellow (Gould et al., 2004).

The basic meaning of the treadmill is strenuous, routine work and effort. To remain in place, we must keep running. A person moves and expends energy; if they don't, the belt will carry them away and throw them down. This figuratively illustrates the core principle of the theory. The permanent acceleration of production and consumption is achieved through the intensive use of natural resources and is associated with growing environmental externalities. The balancing of trends, where every economic slowdown is immediately addressed by pro-growth policies and incentives, as seen during the COVID-19 pandemic, is the essence of the system.

Schnaiberg further argued that the boom in science and technology, which gradually led to the replacement of much human labour by machines, simultaneously created pressure to increase production. The reason for this is that, unlike labour costs, which can be relatively easily reduced by introducing machines, the costs of the machines themselves are only profitable with a substantial increase in production. This trend has two effects: first, it decreases job opportunities; second, it results in a constant increase in production and consumption, accompanied by the depletion of natural resources and an increase in waste. Technology and machines require far more energy and chemicals, and far fewer people, than previous labour-intensive production processes (Schnaiberg 1980, Gould et al. 2004).

The mass deployment of machinery and new technologies in production is, to some extent, slowed in regions like Central Europe by the relatively low cost of labour. However, demographic shifts and rising living expenses are altering these factors, and we will see increasing investments, boosted by new opportunities provided by artificial intelligence.

Data on increasing labour productivity, declining employment, rising resource consumption, and mass production of goods indicate similar trends and development patterns across the globe. According to treadmill theory, as production increases, the availability of investment capital also increases. This leads to further investments in modernising production using new machines and technologies. In essence, a closed cycle of investment is created, and the subsequent need to increase production and sales becomes necessary to recoup these investments and generate profit.

The cycle runs into two problems. First, there are the already mentioned ecological limits of resources and climate change. Second, there is the capacity of the market to absorb the increasing volume of products. This is a classic problem of overproduction.

To some extent, countries usually manage to increase product sales due to economic growth associated with rising wages. But after a certain point, this is no longer sufficient. Then, globalisation and international pressure intervene. Countries are gradually forced to open their markets to international trade. As Buttel (2003) notes, this significant shift in the geographical focus of analysis was not part of Schnaiberg's original theory. We will revisit this aspect with David Harvey later in the book.

The key concept in the treadmill is that increasing production requires the stimulation of consumption. Building on psychology, and with the help of sophisticated marketing strategies, artificial desires and consumerism are created as the main motives of success and life. In the past, the economic goals of countries were mostly centred on meeting the needs of people, especially the wealthy. The goal is no longer to satisfy consumption but to create it, with efforts to constantly reduce costs through mechanisation and, later, the robotisation of the production process.

The economy is no longer just a space for the exchange of goods and commodities to satisfy needs. It has become a society of artificially created consumerism, stimulated by capital, which, in order to survive, needs to constantly increase turnover. These changes would not be possible without the mass support of people living in this society.

Culture and human psychology are part of the overall picture. Capitalism has created a social paradigm for understanding the world, where the fulfilment of needs does not exist. Consumption has come to be understood as a measure of quality of life and satisfaction. What we must keep in mind in any discussion about climate change is that the environment and growth limits are not central to this paradigm; rather, they are marginal. This persists despite the growing green marketing and pressures on producers, especially in developed countries, to display the 'sustainability' of their products. The scale of consumption matters more than the type of products we consume. Even the most sustainable products have environmental footprints due to resource extraction, production, and transportation, and we face the rebound effect, where efficiency gains are offset by increased consumption.

The problem is not in making and delivering products but in selling them. Consumption has therefore gradually become socially constructed, stimulated in increasingly sophisticated ways. Or, as Schiller (1996) describes it, material desires are created by producers and supported by a sophisticated machinery of advertising. The scale of consumption needs to be seen in the context of production decisions. It is production that determines consumption by influencing consumer choices, which originate in three main areas: (a) constraints created by previous production decisions, (b) specific decisions about the economic distribution of goods, and (c) the distribution of decision-making powers and policy-making (Gould et al. 2004: 300).

The transformation of socially constructed material desires into human needs is the result of processes that are strongly influenced by those who decide on production. In opposition to classical and neo-classical economic theories, which claim that it is customer choices that decide the market, there is the argument that these choices are guided by industry. The 'gospel of mass consumption' is a successful construction of customer desires, not an expression of customers themselves but directed by the captains of industry and the advertising sector working alongside them (Gould et al. 2004: 301).

Socially created consumption and the economic interests of producers do not exclude the role of other variables that directly or indirectly come into play. According to Barbosa (2009), these can include culture, ideology, wealth, or boredom. Or, as Sennett (2006) puts it, industry mainly works with our imagination and our striving to achieve something greater. For example, the illusion of owning an expensive all-terrain car and conquering the Sahara, while in reality, people drive their children to school in traffic jams. A larger and more powerful laptop with expensive software, while we are not able to use more than basic functions, which are also available in the previous version or even for free.

Mass consumption, created by industrial production and arising from the transformation of the economy, gradually became a sophisticated and complex phenomenon. Today, we can even say that it has become a kind of substitute space for freedom and self-realisation. In increasingly unfree workplace conditions and the growing stress of job insecurity, the freedom to choose goods is one of the last freedoms we have. Many of our consumer behaviour patterns play with these desires and our psychology and are artificially created by industry, even if we do not admit it or are unaware of it.

The treadmill of production has also found ways to influence our social relations, shaped by social inequalities and competition. Here, we refer to status and positional consumption.

Status consumption is a concept introduced over a century ago by American economist Thorstein Veblen (1899). According to him, in a society where formal hierarchical signs of class are obscured, consumption is one of the ways to earn respect and avoid unfavourable comparisons.

The writer Kálmán Mikszáth describes in his novella *Saint Peter's Umbrella* how the carriage of a successful lawyer looked in the nineteenth-century Austro-Hungarian Empire. A well-kept harness and good horses heralded the owner's success far and wide. Today's equivalent is the passenger car. The model and price of the car serve as symbols. Similarly, a mobile phone. The classic symbolic act of expressing status consumption is the commonly seen act of placing car keys and mobile phones on the table. It is not only important to have them but also to show that I have them.

Positional consumption is a more recent concept introduced by economist Fred Hirsch (1977). According to Hirsch, consumption in modern society has shifted from meeting basic needs to consumption relative to others. In other words, it is not important what I have, but what others have. If the majority, or everyone, has a certain thing, it loses its value. In addition to the environmental limits of growth, Hirsch raises the question of social limits. The result of positional consumption is the permanent frustration of individual expectations. This is due to the cost of consumption, which affects the quality of life, and secondarily, the frustration with the established hierarchy, which provides socially scarce goods only to those on the highest rung of the social ladder, thus permanently undermining the expectations of those who strive to climb this imaginary ladder (Hirsch 1977). Things transform from objects of desire into necessities, but at the same time, their value changes. If we all want to spend our holidays on the 'virgin' Greek islands, they won't stay virgin for long, nor will they elevate our social position.

Psychology, social inequalities, competition, and culture are just a few of the possible explanatory frameworks for what drives mass consumption, propelled by the treadmill of production. The logic of growth and capital is combined here with many human characteristics, giving rise to new forms of expression. But it is about trying to understand what is the cause and what is the effect.

The way we attempt to solve the environmental effects of mass consumption highlights a fundamental paradox. Greening production and consumption has produced some limited positive effects, but these are quickly offset. We face a situation where global incomes are generally rising, and ecological modernisation leads to phenomena like the Jevons paradox and the N-curve. Reducing emissions through technological changes does not necessarily result in an overall decrease in emissions.

In his study, American sociologist G. A. Gonzales (2001) analysed policies aimed at reducing air pollution in California. These policies support technological innovations, such as the development of more energy-efficient car engines, which subsequently reduce air pollution. However, these policies are driven more by financial interests than by environmental ones, despite their positive effects on reducing fossil fuel consumption. Although the approach has had some success, technological improvements have been slower than anticipated, and the total amount of emissions has not decreased – in fact, it has increased. As the operational costs of vehicles have decreased, the number of cars on the roads has grown, as has the average annual distance travelled. Cars have simply become cheaper to own and operate. Gonzales further notes that it would be far more effective to implement changes in spatial planning. However, this is not happening because such changes would require structural and behavioural shifts and would challenge the vested interests of car manufacturers, who are propelled by the treadmill of production.

The Californian example illustrates the Jevons paradox, which is crucial for understanding the limits of green growth. In 1865, English economist William Stanley Jevons wrote *An Inquiry Concerning the Progress of the Nation, and the Probable Exhaustion of Our Coal Mines*. He attempted to predict trends in coal use in England, as many were concerned about the potential exhaustion of this critical resource. Based on his analysis of trends, Jevons concluded that the economy built on cheap coal would decline because neither new technologies nor alternative energy sources would be able to replace coal. He predicted that coal would become increasingly scarce, and its price would rise according to classical economic theories.

From today's perspective, it is clear that Jevons was fundamentally wrong. The technology of the time did not allow for accurate quantification of coal reserves, and he underestimated the possibilities of cheap imports from other countries or the transfer of production to new sources. Above all, he had no idea – as no one did at the time – that oil and natural gas would one day provide industrial companies with much cheaper and more efficient energy sources.

However, what has endured from Jevons' work is the so-called Jevons paradox. Increased efficiency in the use of a particular natural resource (such as coal or oil) does not lead, as might be expected, to a decrease in consumption but rather to its increase. It is a paradox: for example, the more efficient the process of burning coal in the production of a product, the cheaper that product becomes, leading to higher consumption and greater attractiveness for further investments in its production. Increased efficiency and consumption stimulate economic growth, which, in turn, drives further demand.

The Jevons paradox has many applications in the current debate on climate change. If we increase the efficiency of internal combustion engines in cars and reduce gasoline consumption, cars become more economically advantageous. They become more affordable because operational costs are falling. As a result, more people can afford them, and the idea of reducing the ecological impact of cars becomes questionable. Even if we replace combustion engines with electric cars, we still need to produce more vehicles and generate more energy. The more successful we are in reducing the costs of electric vehicles through economies of scale, the more of these cars will be produced and sold, necessitating more energy and resources for their manufacture and use.

Jänicke (2008) describes such effects using a curve in the shape of the letter 'N', or the N-curve. The initial improvement in environmental efficiency is subsequently nullified – or even exceeded – by a later increase in pollution. He cites Japan as an example, where between 1973 and 1985 there was a significant increase in production efficiency and a simultaneous reduction in the consumption of natural resources. However, these positive impacts were neutralised by industrial growth and mass-scale production during the same period.

The treadmill of production, with its internal logic, demands a constant increase in production and consumption, while addressing climate change requires a radical reduction in material and energy use. This does not mean that the treadmill is static or eternally tied to fossil fuels. On the contrary, significant progress has been made through ecological modernisation in reducing environmental externalities in many aspects of product manufacturing, use, and recycling. However, within the global system built on the vision of economic growth modelled on the Northern way of life, tackling climate change is like chasing a moving target. Any progress in reducing greenhouse gas emissions is offset by the ever-increasing global scale of production and consumption.

3.5. Creative Destruction in the Era of Neoliberalism

Transformation is a permanent feature of capitalism, but it can lead to very different outcomes. While Karl Marx viewed the process primarily through the lens of wealth accumulation (Marx 2020, 2023), Joseph Schumpeter described it as 'a process of industrial mutation which continually overturns the economic structure from within, continually destroys the old one, and continually creates a new one' (Schumpeter 2021). Schumpeter coined this process 'creative destruction', emphasising that the old must make way for the new, which better adapts to the needs of capital and provides fresh opportunities for prosperity.

Schumpeter (2021) argued that innovation and technological change are critical drivers of economic evolution. However, the same process of replacing old methods with new ones ultimately undermines and threatens to destroy the capitalist structure itself. Using the metaphor of creative destruction, decarbonisation can be seen as just another episode in the ongoing upheaval of economic structures from within, with the market eventually establishing a new equilibrium.

In the post-WWII history of Europe, the 'new' was often better than the 'old'. We achieved higher levels of social and environmental protection, and new industries became cleaner and far more efficient. However, this does not automatically mean that the creative destruction of the fossil fuel-based economy will lead to a more socially and environmentally friendly future.

Contrary to popular narratives about the 'invisible hand' of the market and the supposed natural evolution of capitalism, studies of industrial evolution – from early England to latecomer South Korea – highlight the central role that states play in facilitating transformation (Gerschenkron 1962, Wade 1990, Hobsbawm 1999, Smith 2001). The state acts as an agent of compromise between the needs of capital owners and the labour force. Earlier stages of industrialisation, arising from creative destruction, were promoted by governments focused on wealth creation, economic development, and competition with other nations. These transformations occurred within frameworks of strong state power, capable of creating favourable conditions for the 'new' while maintaining some degree of social peace.

Today, the narratives surrounding decarbonisation emphasise creative destruction as an essential precondition for mitigating climate change and ensuring the survival of humanity (Murphy 2021, IPCC 2023). However, these narratives often lack a coherent vision of what the 'new' should look like in a world where states increasingly act as agents of neoliberal ideology and global competitiveness. The anticipated closure of coal mines and the transformation of industries tied to fossil fuels should create decarbonised economies. Yet, this economic transformation is occurring in the context of weakened states, facing rapidly growing economic and social problems and widening disparities.

The key question is how much the EU and member state policy pressures and spending on developing decarbonised, decentralised economic structures can lead to viable, sustainable new models. Creative destruction faces structural obstacles embedded within the advancing neoliberal state. Attempts at successful economic transformation on national or regional levels are constrained by global and regional competition (such as the European Single Market) and an institutional framework emphasising public spending cuts, deregulation, and laissez-faire principles.

Decarbonisation can be analysed as a process through which a territory substantially transforms its economic and social systems by downsizing or closing fossil fuel-based industries and transitioning to decarbonised production and consumption patterns. This 'creative destruction' involves targeted interventions across various governance levels, the redirection of private investments, the harnessing of market forces, and stakeholder engagement. The success of this process depends on numerous external and internal factors, and decarbonisation may either positively or negatively influence the well-being and welfare of people.

Bob Jessop argues that regional development disparities and the decline of certain regions are primarily due to the neoliberal restructuring of the economy, the state, and its policies (Jessop 2023). This is particularly true for decarbonisation, where state-led projects are radically reshaping the economic structure of regions within a short period. While creative destruction can happen quickly, the subsequent recovery or 'resurrection' may take decades – or may not occur at all.

The decarbonisation policies of the European Union and its member states are driven by commitments outlined in the Paris Agreement and the European Green Deal, which aims to achieve carbon neutrality by 2050. The Green Deal envisions a 25-year timeline to transform Europe's industrial sector and value chains, emphasising the transition to a climate-neutral and circular economy. However, from an economic and social perspective, this transformation is based on maintaining the status quo and avoiding deeper engagement with the root causes of rising inequalities. The focus remains on planning and compensations.

This transformation, supported by both EU and national governments, relies on redirecting and optimising existing financial instruments alongside newly established initiatives like the Just Transition Mechanism (JTM). Through the JTM, EU member states prioritise regions for piloting Regional Decarbonisation Action Plans and accelerate the implementation of decarbonisation policies. Initial efforts focus on phasing out coal mining and transforming large carbon-intensive industries, which currently provide relatively well-paid jobs.

Unlike past instances of creative destruction, often driven from the bottom up in response to changing conditions, the green transformation is being orchestrated from the top down. The rise of a distinct low-carbon policy represents an ideological state-level project (Wei 2021). This project aims to steer economic transformation but faces limitations due to the prevailing forces shaping the global economy, local structural conditions, and the inability of appeals to a 'just transition' to generate broad public support. The green transformation, as an ideological state-level project, clashes with the broader context of neoliberalism, or the neoliberal state, as the dominant form of political arrangement. Creative destruction is taking place in a completely different environment compared to the era when Europe's social and environmental agendas were first developed.

Neoliberalism is generally characterised by market-oriented reform policies aimed at deregulating capital markets, eliminating price controls, and decreasing trade barriers. The overarching goal is to minimise state influence in the economy, particularly through privatisation and austerity measures. As Cerny and Evans (2001) point out, the neoliberal state focuses on disempowering itself from within regarding a range of key tasks and roles in the face of globalisation. In this context, industries such as mining and heavy manufacturing – those first in line for green transformation – are relics of the past. Centralised mass production with organised labour, which enjoyed decades of special relationships with the state and protection as strategic industries, is increasingly incompatible with the neoliberal framework.

Industries facing creative destruction are losing their traditional protections as governance structures shift toward market-oriented models. However, the emergence of new economic structures remains uncertain in a context of embedded financial orthodoxy and weak or missing industrial policies at the micro-level, all while markets are exposed to global competition.

In Central Europe, this process is exacerbated by what Cerny and Evans (2001) describe as the flexibilisation of the state apparatus and the creation of a 'contractual post-socialist state'. The neoliberal state differs from the welfare state by promoting increased marketisation, liberalising cross-border movements, re-commodifying labour, and privatising public services. Contrary to the post-WWII emphasis on Keynesian policies and addressing market imperfections, the neoliberal perspective builds on some version of Schumpeterian workfare post-national regimes (Jessop 2023) – in other words, an exploitative system that forces people into low-wage or precarious jobs without addressing systemic issues like job availability or fair wages.

How successful this creative destruction will be in Central Europe depends not only on internal structural conditions – shaped by history, industrialisation, and the neoliberalisation of the state – but also on global shifts in production and consumption patterns. It depends on deeper processes of capital accumulation and investment flows, as well as the ability of countries to generate public support for what is essentially an ideological state-level project, driven by the serious threats posed by advancing climate change.

3.6. Challenges of the Welfare State

The tendency to find a compromise between capital and labour, which in the twentieth century led to various models of the welfare state, did not emerge out of nowhere. It was a reaction to fascism in the West and socialist revolutions in Eastern Europe. Through its universalist principles, welfare state measures helped eradicate extreme poverty and enabled unprecedented social mobility. These facts seem to be frequently overlooked by today's theorists and practitioners of the neoliberal state, who often advocate breaking social ties in the name of imaginary competitiveness.

It is increasingly clear that any serious attempt to tackle climate change will incur significant economic and social costs – not only globally but also within the EU and Central European countries. Any viable alternative to the treadmill of production and laissez-faire capitalism will need to provide fairness, redistribution, and social insurance. This requires more than end-of-pipe individual compensations; it demands a general framework accepted by and beneficial to the majority. A discussion on lessons learned and the future of the welfare state vis-à-vis the climate crisis is, therefore, an important step in this direction.

We rely here on a broad definition of the welfare state as a system with three basic characteristics. First, it reduces inequalities and promotes equal opportunities through the redistribution of wealth. Second, it compensates for external impacts that are not included in the direct costs of generating profits (such as social and environmental externalities). Lastly, it reduces social risks, thereby improving quality of life.

Is the welfare state irrelevant, an obstacle, or, conversely, a prerequisite for systemic environmental changes? The welfare state was created as a bulwark against the destructive forces of market society. It acts as a safety net for those who, for various reasons, do not have a direct share in the generated profits. It is the outcome of long – and in many countries, bloody – struggles for the redistribution of resources, which are key to equalising opportunities and enabling the integration of the majority into society.

Redistribution is based on the principles of equal opportunities and the mitigation of disadvantages. It can also be viewed from the practical standpoint of sharing costs and profits. Profits are largely produced with the help of people who are not directly involved in their creation. For instance, the cost of educating the workforce is typically not paid by employers, though they benefit from it. The health of workers heavily relies on public health programmes. Moreover, profits for some may mean losses for others. The establishment of a chemical plant in a coastal region is viewed differently from the perspective of its owners and from that of fishermen or tourism industry workers. The welfare state compensates for and balances these differences, reducing the external social and environmental impacts of the production and consumption systems in a market society.

Through redistribution, education levels, health conditions, and quality of life have improved. At the same time, society has become more democratic. The rise in social status has allowed people from less privileged backgrounds to access schools, offices, and decision-making processes. The power of economic elites has been weakened through elected representatives of the people.

We may debate with Boris Groys (2010) whether the welfare state was 'merely the result of measures to prevent mass uprisings, counter the communist threat, and avoid the total expropriation of the wealthy classes, supported only as long as the fear of communism was acute, and the bourgeoisie was willing to pay significant taxes to pacify the masses and avert the communist threat'. The revolts in Western Europe in the 1960s demonstrate that this was not an unfounded concern. However, it is clear that the fall of centrally planned socialist regimes in Eastern Europe placed increased pressure on the Western European welfare state, as the threat of an alternative – or at least the illusion of it – disappeared.

The roots of the ideas on which the welfare state is built can be traced back long before the emergence of centrally planned state socialism in Central Europe. Ultimately, this socialism stems from the same historical search for solutions to social conflict as the Western European welfare state.

Defining the concept of the welfare state itself is complicated. There are various nuances regarding the foundations on which it developed and was modified in different countries. States do not all use a single social model, and there are several types of welfare states in Europe.

The Scandinavian model is the result of a corporate agreement among major social actors and is based on universalist principles and high taxes. In England, the foundation is the right to a certain quality of life, which can be redefined and adjusted according to the state's needs. The former system in centrally planned socialist economies did not refer to itself as a welfare state (the concept was considered capitalist), but it essentially relied on the universalist redistribution of profits from state-owned production and service sectors.

What these models have in common is that post-WWII development and prosperity were built on them to a great extent. They share several main characteristics: the state assumes political responsibility for employment levels and conditions; social protection is designed for all citizens and built on social inclusion and democracy. The main elements typically include universal healthcare, free higher education, strong labour protections and regulations, and generous welfare programmes in areas such as unemployment insurance, retirement pensions, and public housing.

After the collapse of centrally planned socialism and the advancement of neoliberalism from West to East, the shared vision of the welfare state has begun to crack. This is visible in environmental and climate policies, which increasingly operate with vague concepts, and where the social costs of the green transformation are treated as individual problems.

The proclaimed goal of the Environment Action Programme to 2030 – the EU's common agenda for environmental policy – is to achieve 'living well within planetary boundaries'. This vague definition was later adopted for the European Green Deal and the 2050 targets for climate neutrality. It is symptomatic that debates over what 'living well' practically means sometimes refer to the European social model, and at other times, they focus on compensations – such as for those struggling with high energy prices. The elephant in the room is the neoliberal transformation, which has erased many achievements of social progress in Europe and shifted the debate about the social dimension of climate change from a holistic approach to the individualisation of risk and solutions.

The relationship between the welfare state and the environment is complex. Some critics, like Matthew Paterson (2007), argue that ecological goals and those of a welfare state based on a capitalist system of production are at odds. Over time, the welfare state began to support profit creation by encouraging mass production and consumption.

In this perspective, the system depends on the creation of consumption and the treadmill of production. Here we can return to John Maynard Keynes (1936), who, with his concept of stimulating the economy, created a completely new basis for understanding macroeconomics. One of President George Bush's first appeals after the devastating attacks on the World Trade Center in New York in 2001 was for people to overcome their fear and go shopping. Shopping turns the wheels of production and well-being. As analysed in the previous chapter using Alan Schnaiberg's treadmill theory, success in today's consumer capitalism depends on expanding and selling goods to as many people as possible.

The welfare state helps increase people's purchasing power, not only through overall economic growth and pressure for fairer profit distribution and wage increases but also by guaranteeing support in unemployment, sickness, and old age. This allows people to spend more during their active lives, thereby generating profit for producers of consumer goods. In other words, redistribution democratises and expands consumption. If you do not have to save for school fees or surgery, you can, for example, travel twice a year to Thailand for vacations.

Thanks to Keynesian approaches to stimulating the economy, combined with redistribution, the welfare state was able to spin the wheels of factories, while redistributing surplus value supported the creation of a massive consumer society. Mass production, without fully integrating external environmental costs, dramatically cheapened consumption.

Is the welfare state therefore environmentally harmful, as Paterson (2007) suggests? We argue that it is not, because it is a tool that can be designed and used in different ways. The welfare state arose from a long-term effort for a fairer and safer society, equalising differences and compensating for the external costs of generated profit. The real question is how to change the current setup of the system so that it fulfils these goals without increasing environmental and climate pressures.

For example, why should healthcare be expensive and cars relatively cheap? If we included positive and negative externalities in their prices, it should be exactly the opposite. The challenge is not to dismantle the welfare state but to reform and combine its advantages with an environmental vision of an economy operating within the limits of planetary boundaries.

Instead of naming the real culprits for the gradual trend of declining government revenues, the blame is placed on expensive labour, an ageing population, and high environmental standards that restrict business. Many people working in production or services see the environment as a direct threat. They fear the closing of their factories, the curtailment of business in the service sector, and an overall decline in employment. A myth is being created that, to maintain today's standard of living, we must sacrifice both social rights and nature, as otherwise, we have no chance of succeeding in global competition. This narrative tries to sell us social instability, increasing risks, and a deteriorating environment as the outcomes of an expensive welfare state. As a reward, we are promised relatively higher incomes – if we happen to be healthy, of productive age, and employed.

Economies and GDP have grown unevenly but consistently over the past decades, and incomes have been increasing. Businesses have become wealthier, while there is greater pressure to cut public spending. The discourse has shifted from striving for a socially just society to liberating the market, which is expected to bring prosperity. The question is, when? Demographic trends exist, the cost of medical technology is rising, and state expenses are increasing. Yet, taxes – which are traditionally the main source of income for the welfare state – are systematically reduced, and tax havens are tolerated. As illustrated in Figure 7, tax revenues in Central Europe declined at the beginning of the 1990s transformation and, despite some fluctuations, have never returned to previous levels.

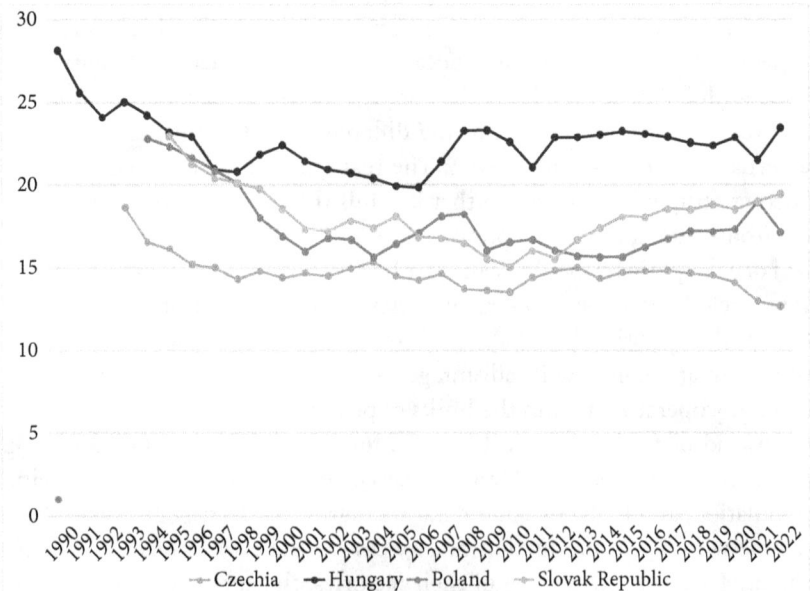

Figure 7: Tax revenue (% of GDP) in Central European countries.
Source: World Development Indicators, International Monetary Fund, Government Finance Statistics Yearbook and data files, and World Bank and OECD GDP estimates.

Since the second half of the 1990s, corporate taxes (income taxes for legal entities) in Europe have been continuously and sharply declining – from an average of 35.3 % in 1995 to 23.2 % in the 2000s. Standard corporate tax rates are 25.8 % in the Netherlands, 25 % in France or Spain, 19 % in the Czech Republic or Poland, and 21 % in Slovakia, with no country planning to increase them.

Furthermore, globalised capital no longer respects national borders and pays taxes wherever it is most advantageous – if it pays them at all. A study by the Government Accountability Office in 2008 found that almost 70 % of American corporations did not pay any corporate income tax. It is no coincidence that more and more holdings and financial groups in Central Europe are headquartered in Cyprus and other tax havens inside and outside Europe. On one side, there is pressure for efficiency and wage reduction; on the other, astronomical multimillion-dollar rewards and bonuses are paid to management. The result is an increase in social inequality.

We live in what Ulrich Beck (1999) describes as a risk society. Risks have always been an inherent part of human life; however, a certain degree of stability and security is essential for most people. In modern industrial society, the notions of stability and security evolved into goals of social struggle for a fairer redistribution of profits and the creation of mechanisms to address the challenges of an atomised society driven by economic growth. This struggle gave rise to the welfare state, which emerged as a response to perceived risks while simultaneously proving beneficial to capitalism.

New forms of production and consumption demanded a different type of workforce. The welfare state played a crucial role in this transformation by fostering education and independence, which supported social mobility and increased the supply of a qualified labour force. Moreover, it legitimised capitalism as a democratic system, making it not only more appealing to its own citizens but also an attractive model globally. The welfare state – or its future modification – may also play a crucial role in shaping a new social vision for a decarbonised, climate-neutral economy.

In this context, it is notable that while contemporary EU strategies and policy documents frequently emphasise the importance of ensuring a 'just' and 'fair' green transformation, they carefully avoid addressing issues related to taxation, redistribution, or the future of the welfare state.

3.7. Ecological Modernisation as the Universal Answer

Although modern political systems based on capitalism and industrialism were inherently anti-ecological, they are undergoing important transformations – both in their overarching narratives and in specific technological and managerial solutions. The reasons for this lie in a complex mix of historical factors, real pollution-related problems, health concerns, the rising cost of resources, and the necessity to respond to various global and local pressures.

Consequently, the main effort of environmentalists should be to push for both the extent and depth of these changes (Eckersley, 2004). The key question, however, is where the limits of the system lie. The intertwined logic of global geopolitics, as analysed by the school of realism, and the logic of capital growth and accumulation – the systemic imperatives of capitalism – create structural barriers that effectively prevent the radical changes required for climate neutrality. Even if we assume that the European Green Deal, with its 2040 and 2050 targets, can withstand increasing opposition from across the political spectrum, the financial and social costs could be enormous. The pathway adopted might ultimately prove unrealistic and incompatible with the system itself.

Some, like Arthur Mol (2000), view the institutional and social changes seen since the 1980s as more than mere cosmetic adjustments, arguing that they represent a structural transformation of industrial society and its institutional order. However, can we not also analyse the relative progress in decarbonisation – what we observe in practice – as something largely built on maintaining the status quo? Progress continues as long as it keeps the system intact, ensures plausible returns on investment, and does not undermine general profitability. This is where support for green investments, green management, or technological solutions as structural responses to climate and environmental challenges originates.

In this book, we use the term ecological modernisation, which is defined as a theoretical approach and policy framework that suggests environmental protection and economic growth can be mutually reinforcing rather than conflicting. It is based on the premise that technological advancements, market-based solutions, and institutional reforms can drive sustainability and environmental improvements within capitalist economies. Since ecological modernisation remains a dominant paradigm in environmental policy – shaping the EU Green Deal, Sustainable Development Goals (SDGs), and global corporate sustainability strategies – it deserves critical examination.

The concept of ecological modernisation emerged in the early 1980s in Germany and quickly gained popularity in many countries (Jänicke, 2008). It functions as both an analytical approach and a political strategy in environmental discussions (Hajer, 1995). It builds on the assumption that we can generate growth – or at least preserve the status quo – without increasing environmental impacts. Instead, it envisions their stabilisation and gradual reduction through emissions reductions and minimising environmental harm. Economically, this represents the decoupling of economic growth from environmental degradation, creating a model of sustainability based on the internalisation of externalities and the sustainable management of natural resources.

Ecological modernisation illustrates many of the paradoxes found within capitalism and its internal mechanisms for addressing environmental problems. The premise that we can redefine the relationship between economic growth and ecology may prove short-lived. The idea that we can sustain economic growth while reducing environmental impacts through constant innovation (Spaargaren & Mol, 1992; Mol, 2000) assumes that we can change production and consumption through gradual transformation, without disrupting capitalism's fundamental reliance on increasing production, consumption, and economic growth. While we may emphasise recycling, reuse, dematerialisation, and efficiency improvements, the underlying mantra of economic growth remains unchallenged.

A final goal of gradual transformation is a closed-loop economy, which Paul Hawken (1999) calls Natural Capitalism. Through ecological modernisation, productivity should increase, which in turn should finance the transformation of industry into a biological model of a closed cycle with zero waste. This involves shifting from selling goods to providing services while reinvesting in natural capital, which would secure future prosperity.

Ecological modernisation is both a research-driven and innovation-promoting approach to solving environmental problems. Unlike direct emission reduction efforts, it encompasses a broad range of eco-innovation measures. It promotes market-based and economic solutions, such as reducing material intensity, implementing eco-design, expanding recycling, and dematerialising consumption. This involves creating new products and production processes that consume fewer natural resources and generate less environmental impact. Concepts such as industrial ecology, industrial metabolism, and green consumption are all based on this theoretical framework.

The approach also combines economic and environmental arguments. By consuming less energy, using cleaner technologies, and reducing raw material use, cost savings are generated. This is the basis for the so-called win-win strategy, where protecting nature and increasing profitability are achieved simultaneously. Additionally, the eco-design of products ensures they require fewer harmful materials and are easier to recycle. More broadly, ecological modernisation aims to influence behaviour, values, and lifestyles, mirroring the logic of increasing labour productivity – maximising output while minimising resource inputs and waste.

Research also focuses on the role of government and businesses in promoting ecological modernisation, their capabilities and motivations in accelerating structural changes, and the optimal mix of legislative and market-based instruments. Political, cultural, and economic factors influencing the adoption or resistance to eco-innovations are investigated, and substantial resources are allocated to technological and management research.

Ecological modernisation has gained widespread popularity among businesses and politicians because it reduces costs, facilitates compliance with environmental regulations, and is politically uncontroversial. It does not demand systemic change or challenge market mechanisms. Instead, it assumes that solutions are technical and technological and can be implemented through market forces.

From the perspective of mainstream environmental politics, ecological modernisation is the dominant ideological foundation of climate change policies. While individual innovations yield incremental improvements, the overall effectiveness of ecological modernisation in solving complex environmental crises remains debatable.

Capitalism must continue investing and growing to survive, a process explained by David Harvey's (2010) key concepts such as overaccumulation, the growth imperative, creative destruction, and profit rates. When capital accumulates beyond profitable investment opportunities, economic stagnation occurs unless new markets emerge. Green technologies and decarbonisation investments fit within this framework, but their success depends on profitability.

At best, ecological modernisation enables moderate progress toward decarbonisation. However, the falling rate of profit – a central concern in Marxist economics – forces capitalists to maintain profitability through outsourcing, cost-cutting, technological innovation, or financialisation. Creative destruction, therefore, is not a loss, but an investment opportunity – for instance, replacing coal boilers with heat pumps generates profit.

However, the core criticism of green growth is that it does not address the system's organisation or the nature of profit generation. The rebound effect remains a key challenge: efficiency gains often lead to greater overall consumption, offsetting environmental benefits and reinforcing Jevons' paradox. For example, while we can modernise car production to reduce emissions or switch to electric vehicles, the total number of cars continues to grow, increasing the environmental impact of their production.

Ecological modernisation may progress if it is supported by a gradually strengthening policy and legislative framework. However, this comes at the cost of a diminishing rate of return on old investments, only partially replaced by returns from new investment areas. The policy and legislative framework would need to be globally accepted to prevent free riders and price dumping. Some attempts have worked within relatively homogeneous regions, such as Europe with its single market, but on a global level, such coordination remains largely a fantasy.

The main challenge is affordability. Transitioning to a green, decarbonised economy is neither easy nor cheap. Technical solutions and super-industrialisation require substantial investments in science and research, which are crucial for competitiveness and provide countries with a comparative advantage. The vision of a green economy is based on the assumption that long-term economic growth will generate enough resources to finance modern technologies and reduce environmental pressure. However, is it realistically possible to achieve a super-industrial economy based on advanced, carbon-neutral technologies on a global scale?

According to Buttel (2000), green growth, as a derivative of modernisation theories, is only applicable to a small group of countries that have developed according to classical modernisation patterns. It is barely applicable to developing countries and instead serves core economies to maintain or widen their technological head start. Finally, even if modernisation and climate crisis mitigation policies progress globally and generate sufficient profit rates, they may still arrive too late from a climate perspective. Here, we can argue that ecological modernisation does not challenge the fundamental growth-driven nature of capitalism, which may be inherently unsustainable. This brings us to a central conflict of environmental policy: economic expansion versus ecological limits.

Techno-optimism and over-reliance on technology as a solution to ecological problems may ignore deeper systemic issues, such as overconsumption and inequality, but also the crucial issue of time. In theory, market pressures and legislative modifications should drive technological progress, and industries should gradually adopt modern approaches. The energy sector, in particular, could undergo radical transformation. However, early adopters of new technology often face disadvantages compared to those who continue using older, already paid-off technologies. The solution would require legislative intervention and economic incentives from the state. However, corporations actively resist such changes. From a cost-benefit perspective, companies find it more advantageous to extend the lifespan of existing technologies or incrementally improve environmental parameters, rather than replacing entire systems with expensive new ones. In a global economy without enforceable environmental standards, loopholes and regulatory arbitrage further delay transitions. These delays are critical, given that time is a decisive factor in mitigating climate change.

That being said, it is still better to pursue ecological modernisation than to do nothing at all. In certain sectors, such as renewable energy, modernisation has undoubtedly been successful. However, when examining global developments across different regions, economic progress is generally accompanied by increasing greenhouse gas emissions. Fossil fuel consumption continues to grow, with environmental externalities accumulating at every stage of the production cycle – from raw material extraction to processing and waste management. Household emissions and changing consumption patterns add further pressure. A vast body of literature, international reports, and research from both governmental and non-governmental organisations underscores the acceleration of environmental crises, leading to climate change and the irreversible degradation of ecosystems.

Despite these challenges, quality of life indicators such as education levels, material well-being, and life expectancy have improved in most regions over recent decades. When analysing global trends, we observe an increase in overall well-being occurring alongside environmental decline (MEA, 2005). For instance, the Human Development Index (HDI) – which tracks literacy, life expectancy, and average income – has shown steady improvement since the 1970s for both developing and developed countries. This presents what could be termed a 'climate paradox':

Why, despite the expansion of green investments and an improving global quality of life, have we failed to effectively address climate change?

One caveat is how quality of life is measured. The basic parameters used in global assessments may not fully capture reality. For many people, actual living conditions may be deteriorating. Residents of New Delhi or Bangkok, for example, may be financially better off than a decade ago, but they now endure severe air pollution, driven by fossil fuel dependence. They also face rising healthcare costs, exacerbating their hardships. Among the most critical ecosystem services influencing quality of life is food production. Thus, if per capita food production increases, this is statistically recorded as an improvement in quality of life, even if other ecosystem services deteriorate.

Moreover, while quality of life improves for some, it does not mean it will improve for everyone, nor that it will continue improving. The key question is: Who benefits now, and who will benefit in the future? The mainstream political narrative insists that we can tackle climate change while improving quality of life globally, without disrupting the capitalist system. Inequalities are presented as natural, and we are told that rising tides lift all boats.

Yet, if we examine global emissions trends (Figure 8), the picture is far from encouraging. Despite massive investments in greening economies, global greenhouse gas emissions continue to rise. Emissions have been increasing since the Industrial Revolution, and the 1992 Framework Convention on Climate Change has failed to reverse this trend. China's emissions growth is particularly striking. However, it is crucial to recognise that China's emissions are largely driven by manufacturing goods for the rest of the world. The EU is a global leader in emission reduction, but it remains far from achieving climate neutrality.

If we consider emissions on a cumulative global scale, they continue to rise, despite decades of climate policies and international agreements. According to IPCC projections, emissions are likely to keep increasing – even under optimistic scenarios.

Annual CO$_2$ emissions

Carbon dioxide (CO$_2$) emissions from fossil fuels and industry [1]. Land-use change is not included.

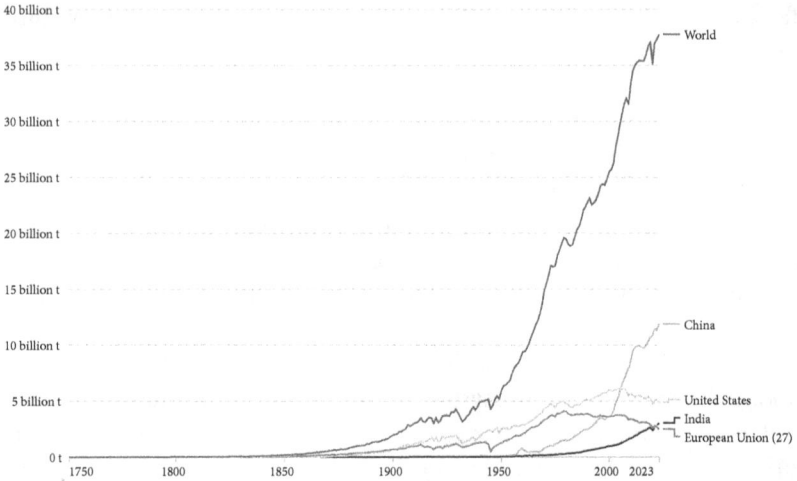

1. Fossil emissions : Fossil emissions measure the quantity of carbon dioxide (CO$_2$) emitted from the burning of fossil fuels, and directly from industrial processes such as cement and steel production. Fossil CO$_2$ includes emissions from coal, oil, gas, flaring, cement, steel, and other industrial processes. Fossil emissions do not include land use change, deforestation, soils, or vegetation.

Data source: Global Carbon Budget (2024)

OurWorldinData.org/co2-and-greenhouse-gas-emissions | CC BY

Figure 8: Cumulative CO$_2$ emissions globally and in the EU, USA, India and China (1750–2023).
Source: Hannah Ritchie, Pablo Rosado and Max Roser (2023) – 'CO$_2$ and Greenhouse Gas Emissions' Published online at OurWorldinData.org. Retrieved from: <https://ourworldindata.org/co2-and-greenhouse-gas-emissions> [Online Resource]

While the example of the EU demonstrates that some progress can be achieved through the greening of production and consumption, it remains far from sufficient – especially when considering the import of carbon embedded in products and services. The challenges of ecological modernisation can be analysed on multiple levels – economic, technological, social, political, and ecological. While ecological modernisation proposes strategies to integrate environmental sustainability into capitalist systems, it faces inherent limitations that prevent it from fundamentally resolving the environmental crises generated by capitalism.

These limitations stem from the contradictions between the principles of endless economic growth, profit maximisation, and resource extraction – central to capitalism – and the finite nature of Earth's resources and ecosystems. As discussed in other parts of this book, the system relies on continuous economic growth for stability, driven by profit accumulation and market expansion. This growth typically necessitates increasing resource extraction and energy consumption, which directly conflicts with ecological limits. While modernisation offers strategies to mitigate environmental challenges within capitalist frameworks, it encounters substantial barriers that prevent it from fundamentally 'saving' capitalism.

One major issue is the global problem of time. A closer examination reveals that trends in major economic blocs and countries differ significantly. The EU and the USA have been somewhat successful in decoupling their economic growth from emissions. In contrast, emissions continue to rise in India and especially in China. This disparity is further complicated by factors such as the outsourcing of production, historical responsibility, the right to development, and the uneven distribution of negative consequences. The global distribution of production and consumption, as well as profits and losses, creates conflicts between developed, transitional, and developing countries – challenges that ecological modernisation is ill-equipped to address in the short term.

Technological fixes to existing infrastructure often result in more expensive and complex solutions. As Barbosa (2009: 38) notes, this trend reflects 'super-industrialisation'. In contrast to radical approaches that advocate simplification, super-industrialisation attempts to solve complex technical problems through further technological innovations. Ecological modernisation promotes 'green growth', suggesting that technological innovation and efficiency can decouple economic growth from environmental harm. However, evidence shows that absolute decoupling – where economic growth occurs without increasing resource use or emissions – is rare and insufficient to meet global climate goals. This dynamic can even lead to the Jevons paradox, where increased efficiency lowers costs, making products more affordable and thus stimulating greater consumption, ultimately negating environmental benefits.

Ecological modernisation relies heavily on market-based approaches, such as carbon trading, green bonds, and payments for ecosystem services. These mechanisms commodify nature and align closely with concepts of deregulation and privatisation. In this regard, ecological modernisation often harmonises with the gradual neoliberalisation of the state. However, this relationship is not straightforward. Ecological modernisation still requires some active state intervention to set standards, enforce regulations, and incentivise green transitions. Yet effective implementation depends on strong governance frameworks, which neoliberal policies often erode.

3.8. Where is Our Good Old Sustainable Development?

To achieve transformative outcomes, we must move beyond ecological modernisation and neoliberal frameworks by embracing stronger, systemic approaches that address the root causes of environmental degradation and the climate crisis. Are we on the right path? Far from it. Geopolitical competition in a world where capitalism is practically the only economic system does not allow for significant deviations and limits the manoeuvring space for effective climate change policies. As Kilbourne and Carlson (2008) point out, this space is based on the doctrine of political liberalism, private property, and the notion of the market as a space for self-realisation and profit accumulation – with growth and a belief in technical solutions to civilisational challenges as its main goals.

Capitalism is currently under double pressure. On one hand, it is trying to save itself from environmental degradation and climate change, as these issues impose enormous economic and social costs. It must respond to public discourse and stakeholder pressures, which makes some degree of regulation both feasible and acceptable. On the other hand, capitalism is also striving to preserve the structural conditions for its own expansion, conditions based on the logic of deregulation, competitiveness, and growth. The attitudes toward regulation and the level of regulatory tolerance change over time.

These internal conflicts are clearly reflected in public discourse and in how nature protection or climate action is operationalised in visions, strategies, or policies. Words matter. The early discourse on nature protection, limits to growth, and environmental conservation underwent a transformation in the 1990s and was later embodied in public narratives surrounding the green transition, built around the concept of sustainable development – a development that combines environmental, social, and economic concerns while keeping the existing system intact. The breakthrough moment was the United Nations Conference on Environment and Development (UNCED), also known as the Earth Summit, held in Rio de Janeiro, Brazil, in 1992, which significantly influenced transformation narratives for the following decades.

In the spirit of marketing campaigns, it is sometimes beneficial to rebrand a product to revive interest. For instance, instead of 'protection', the term 'sustainability' is now used. However, like in marketing, this change in terminology may reflect deeper motivations. It is therefore useful to examine the discourse and the terms used from a historical perspective – critically analysing their origins, definitions, and anchoring – to understand how terminology can reveal the control of the agenda by dominant economic and social players. In the second half of the twentieth century, discussions about the impact of human activity on the environment and the search for solutions within the system led to efforts to define development goals – visions for harmonising growth and environmental protection, which had previously been understood as antagonistic. The best-known and most promoted outcome of these efforts was the formulation of the concept of sustainable development.

Defining sustainable development has been the subject of ongoing debate. To understand the present, we must go back to its roots. The need to define a vision or direction for development intensified in the 1970s. With the publication of *Limits to Growth* (Meadows et al. 1972), debates about what types of development are possible within given ecosystem limits gained momentum. Sustainability was seen as a balance with basic ecological support systems (Stivers 1976). At the height of influence of new social movements, environmental issues became a central concern for governments and businesses.

In 1987, a commission led by G. H. Brundtland prepared a report for the United Nations titled *Our Common Future*. It provided the most commonly cited definition of sustainable development: development that meets the needs of the present without compromising the ability of future generations to meet their own needs (WCED 1987).

Based on this vague definition, many modifications have emerged. What they have in common is that they scrupulously avoid concrete considerations or proposals for changing the unsustainable dominant paradigm of capitalism. As James O'Connor (1994: 2) argues, sustainability is primarily an ideological and political issue, not just an ecological or economic one. From the beginning, definitions of sustainability were shaped by the 1992 World Earth Summit in Rio de Janeiro, which adopted *Agenda 21*, described as a guide to achieving sustainable development worldwide.

Reports such as *Our Common Future* and *Agenda 21* were significant in mapping environmental challenges. They did not treat the environment as a separate issue but rather as an intersection of economic and social concerns. They formulated a consensus that economic development should align with social development while respecting the planet's environmental limits. With this interdisciplinary approach, sustainable development became institutionalised in policies, plans, and official documents.

Sustainable development strategies were quickly adopted by the European Union, national governments, and even corporations. Not so long ago, in 2001, the EU adopted its Strategy for Sustainable Development (EU SDS), which was renewed in June 2006 with the goal of achieving 'continuous improvement of quality of life for both the present and future generations'.

If we compare the adoption of the European strategy with, for example, the REACH directive on chemical substances, we see a stark contrast – sustainability strategies were implemented smoothly, without significant resistance from business. The reason is simple: strategic materials based on an overly broad definition of sustainable development do not threaten the interests of any powerful groups or lobbies. But why? Is it a flaw in the concept itself, or just its problematic implementation, where the resulting policies are often toothless compromises? The truth likely lies somewhere in between.

The first contradictions in defining sustainable development emerged early on. Is it merely a managerial approach to environmental issues (e.g. ecological modernisation), or does it represent an ideology promoting radical social and economic changes? For some, sustainability is about protecting wetlands or planting trees; for others, it is about progressive taxation and corporate accountability as the foundation for addressing climate change.

Many key theorists and practitioners leaned toward the idea that sustainability should entail a fundamental shift in how we understand concepts such as growth, quality of life, and the provision of basic needs. The more radical, though still system-compatible, ideas suggested transitioning toward degrowth, reducing consumption, or reviving communitarian forms of societal organisation. In this perspective, environmental problems are inherently social problems, and technological solutions are merely tools, not end goals. For instance, while recycling waste is beneficial, it does not challenge the global supply chains and consumption patterns that drive environmental degradation. However, such radical interpretations of sustainable development have always been marginalised – and continue to be.

Calls for addressing environmental degradation and climate change were gradually appropriated by politicians, businesses, think tanks, and the media. Sustainability began to be framed as a gradual transition, avoiding radical interventions. The concept became vague – perhaps intentionally – allowing it to gain widespread acceptance, even from its original opponents.

The incorporation of the sustainability agenda and its transformation into a non-threatening concept illustrates the role of key institutions in shaping environmental and climate policies. Today, international policies are increasingly dominated and influenced by transnational corporations and business interests (Brown et al. 1993, Korten 2001, Judt 2010).

A 2011 study by systems theorists from the Swiss Federal Institute of Technology in Zurich found that a core network of 1,318 companies controls about 60 % of global production, with an even smaller subset of 147 firms controlling 40 % of this entire network. These are primarily financial institutions, such as Barclays, JPMorgan Chase, and Goldman Sachs. According to Leslie Sklair (2000, 2002), such entities have managed to shape and control the global debate on environmental issues, shifting the climate agenda away from activists, the public, and national governments.

Within this dynamic, businesses are not framed as objects of scrutiny but rather as key partners and leaders in environmental action. Sustainability has provided a platform for redefining the discourse. Just as corporations and lobby groups have shaped global economic trends, they have also shaped sustainability narratives. As the saying goes, if you can't beat them, join them. Initially, radical environmental activists opposed industry and politics, but over time, businesses not only engaged in the discussion – they took control of it. Today, no significant policy document dares to question their central role.

By the early 1970s, organisations such as the International Chamber of Commerce (ICC) were already influencing global environmental policy. This role was cemented at the first UN Conference on the Environment in Stockholm (1972) and later reinforced by the World Business Council for Sustainable Development (WBCSD). The WBCSD, founded by Swiss multimillionaire Stephan Schmidheiny, played a leading role at the 1992 Earth Summit in Rio de Janeiro.

As Schmidheiny (2002) stated, 'Environmental protection has long been a defensive, negativist, and regressive concept.' Instead, he and others in the business community pushed for 'sustainable growth' over environmental protection. Leslie Sklair (2000:10) notes that Schmidheiny actively shaped this shift, recognising that 'growth' sounded more progressive than 'protection'.

The fundamental issue with sustainable development is that it has become a vague, feel-good slogan. As O'Connor (1994:1) remarked, 'Sustainability can mean basically anything one wants it to mean, which is why it is so appealing.' In practice, it largely translates into green growth – reliant on technological fixes, market-based solutions, and ecological modernisation. It is deeply embedded in global policy frameworks, most notably through the United Nations' Sustainable Development Goals (SDGs), but it has also become a buzzword that is increasingly diluted and vague.

On one hand, initiatives like the European Green Deal operate on the premise of balancing economic growth, social equity, and environmental protection. Governments, businesses, and civil society now routinely refer to sustainability as a guiding principle for long-term planning and investment. Yet one may argue that this is mainly because the concept has been co-opted by neoliberal agendas, transforming it into a technocratic tool that prioritises 'green growth' rather than challenging the deeper structural issues of inequality, overconsumption, and environmental degradation.

The EU Strategy for Sustainable Development is now more than two decades old. The Green Deal refers to sustainability ninety-five times in its text, claiming that Europe must firmly commit to a new path of sustainable and inclusive growth. By 2024, the EU's sustainability discourse had shifted once again. The European Commission now promotes a framework centred on competitiveness, security, and fairness, relegating environmental and climate concerns to a secondary role. It seems that the sustainability debate has been successfully reframed in a way that ensures business as usual – preserving the core economic structures that continue to drive environmental degradation and bringing us closer to a climate catastrophe.

Challenging System Limits and Central European Dilemmas

When British Prime Minister Clement Attlee and his government introduced public healthcare and social support legislation after World War II, Britain was arguably at its poorest. Today, in much wealthier societies, we are told that social and climate concerns must wait in the interest of economic growth – and, gradually, in the interest of militarisation and preparing for upcoming wars.

At least since the publication of *Limits to Growth* (Meadows et al., 1972), we have known that we are reaching – or even exceeding – the limits of our current system. Data on climate change progress and scenarios are clear: the world is at a crossroads. Although competition and confrontation have always been part of the global order, for the first time in history we are nearing the limits of exploitation and conflict that our planet can support.

In the previous section, we examined the emerging EU framework currently shaping the debate on decarbonisation and climate neutrality. Over the past decades, we have witnessed a significant shift in European green and climate policies – from modest beginnings aimed at preventing dumping to protect the Single European Market to ambitious targets of achieving climate neutrality by 2050. This represents remarkable progress achieved mainly through ecological modernisation. Yet, growing resistance to the Green Deal and increasing geopolitical tensions raise questions: Is this the peak of our effort, or are we already on a descending curve?

In this section, we delve into the deeper structural conditions and external factors that limit Europe – specifically Central Europe – in addressing the systemic challenges imposed by climate change. As highlighted by nearly all the data and indicators discussed in this book, despite progress, we are far from achieving a sustainable future. We are running out of steam in finding leverage points to stay on track, not to mention implementing more radical systemic changes.

In an attempt to address growing internal pressures within the EU, the competitiveness–security–fairness framework was developed and discussed. Climate change remains a critical issue, yet it increasingly takes a back seat. Changing times and public sentiment in Europe are particularly visible in the opposition to the Green Deal, which has increasingly become a symbol – and for some, a scapegoat – for perceived European regression. The world system is never static, and critics often abstract or ignore deeper structural conditions linked to geopolitics, evolving global production and consumption patterns, and demographic decline. For some, the Green Deal represents a new model by which Europe can position itself on future maps as a self-sufficient, climate-neutral economy; for others, it is a matter of either victory and survival in global competition or defeat and decline.

Unsurprisingly, resistance to the Green Deal is particularly fierce in Central Europe, where an economic model based on low wages and manufacturing industries has reached its limits. For decades, the political narrative has been built on progress, growth, and catching up with the 'West'. Countries whose relative prosperity depended on a strong manufacturing base now harbour serious doubts about the future.

The EU's modernisation perspective, as embodied in the Green Deal, is based on the assumption that a reformed version of capitalism – what some call 'green capitalism' or 'sustainable capitalism' – can compete on the global stage while generating enough resources to maintain social welfare, albeit within an increasingly constrained scope. In economic terms, this involves regulating the system, integrating environmental costs into market prices, and using soft tools like agreements, corporate responsibility, and societal shifts to favour sustainability over short-term gains.

Proponents argue that capitalism's mechanisms of innovation and competition can drive the transition to a low-carbon economy. For example, government interventions have stimulated the development of renewable energy technologies, electric vehicles, and energy-efficient solutions. Decreasing costs, growing market demand, and increased private investment have further accelerated this transition. To some extent, this approach works: capital seeks multiplication and growth, and for many investors, a solid rate of return – whether on arms trade or solar panels – makes little difference.

Using the analytical framework of David Harvey, a prominent Marxist geographer and social theorist, we understand that capitalism necessitates continuous investment and growth. Whether investing in harmful chemicals or in recultivating a landfill is secondary to capitalism's internal logic, which is inherently expansionary. According to Harvey, capitalism must keep growing to survive, but this relentless drive for growth eventually clashes with social and environmental limits. The pursuit of profit often leads to exploitation, inequality, and environmental degradation. The system adeptly commodifies natural resources and labour in new ways, effectively delaying – but never overcoming – the impacts of these limits. This relentless need for growth exacerbates social and ecological crises, ultimately leading to instability (Harvey 2010, 2018, 2019).

The Green Deal is largely built on the premise that capitalism can adapt to decarbonisation if the right policies are in place and if the rate of return remains competitive compared to other investment opportunities. Mechanisms such as carbon taxes, emissions trading systems, and green subsidies should incentivise companies to reduce their carbon footprint. Additionally, there is potential to boost 'green finance', where investors prioritise Environmental, Social, and Governance (ESG) criteria. Well-regulated capital markets could reward companies adopting sustainable practices, reflecting a shift in investment strategies toward long-term sustainability over short-term profits.

However, at least three significant challenges complicate this optimistic picture for Central Europe: time, inequality, and geopolitics. First, the inherent focus of capitalism on short-term profits fundamentally clashes with the long-term nature of climate action. Political commitment often depends on immediate donors, while companies prioritise quarterly earnings and shareholder demands, making it difficult to invest in sustainable practices that may take years to become profitable – if they become profitable at all. Firms also tend to externalise environmental costs, meaning that the true cost of carbon emissions is not reflected in the price of goods and services. This creates a situation where polluting is cheaper than adopting clean alternatives, and manufacturing outside the Single European Market brings additional benefits. Central Europe's manufacturing industry is on the front lines of competition. A weak research and development infra-structure for high-end green technologies, combined with dependency on heavy industry, renders the region particularly vulnerable to the impacts of decarbonisation.

Second, these tensions could only be resolved by global agreements, by protecting the European internal market, or by fundamentally restructuring the economy – shifting from manufacturing to services, as many Western counterparts in the EU have done.

Third, the global distribution of production, consumption, profits, and losses creates conflicts among developed, transitional, and developing coun-tries. These conflicts are rooted in historical responsibility and differing perceptions of the right to development. Geopolitical tensions further hinder the global cooperation needed to tackle climate change and effectively prevent the establishment of stronger global rules.

Protecting the European internal market – discussed, for instance, through mechanisms like the Carbon Border Adjustment Mechanism – is of vital interest to many Central European industries. However, it clashes with the expert-driven approach of the European economy. The EU imposed anti-dumping and anti-subsidy measures on Chinese solar panels, wafers, and cells as early as 2013 and experimented with duties on Chinese electric vehicles. While these measures may offer temporary protection, they often fail to address the deeper, structural factors driving China's competitiveness. The industry's global integration allows it to quickly adapt and circumvent such trade barriers – not to mention the countermeasures on European exports that undermine any stronger EU position.

4.1. The Paths to Climate Neutrality and Reality

Central Europe essentially faces three possible scenarios regarding the Green Deal: passive, subversive, and active. In the passive scenario, governments set minimalist goals, mechanically fulfil obligations within the EU frame-work, and place little emphasis on robust implementation. In the subversive scenario, they actively oppose the Green Deal – joining forces with those advocating for its abandonment or revision, postponing and slowing down necessary political and legislative steps, blocking decision-making, and ques-tioning already adopted measures. The active scenario involves shifting from a passive recipient of change to an active co-creator, with a strong emphasis on rapidly transforming the economy by effectively leveraging EU financial instruments.

Projections based on data show that meeting the EU's climate goals for 2030 and 2050 will require extremely strong measures and substantial financing (Figure 9). Achieving climate neutrality will additionally depend on robust regulatory frameworks, incentives for green innovation, and significant shifts in both consumer and investor behaviour. The era of low-hanging fruit is over, and if the EU stays on the path toward neutrality, the costs will increasingly rise. Meanwhile, as the EU framework remains in place, Central Europe appears to be oscillating between the passive and subversive scenarios.

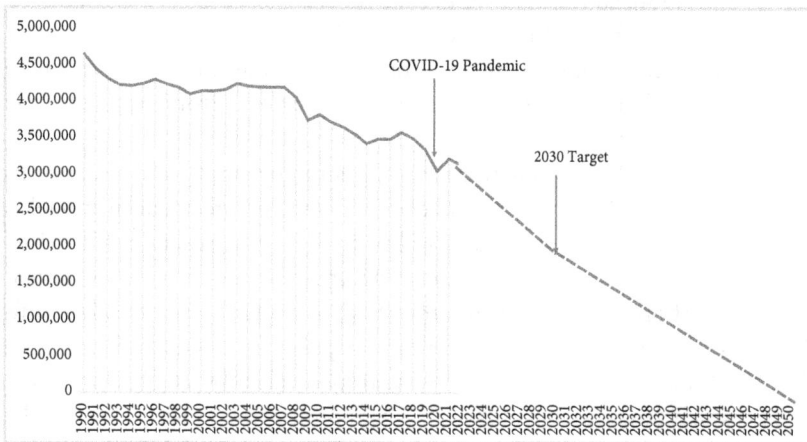

Figure 9: Projection of the necessary trend to meet the EU 27 goals by 2030 and 2050 (kt CO_2 eq).
Source: EEA greenhouse gases – data viewer. Based on data reported by EU Member States under the EU Governance Regulation.

It is fair to say that the Central European position is not an easy one. Beyond the challenges posed by an industrial and manufacturing base, social inequalities present a major hurdle. The unequal distribution of wealth in capitalist economies complicates efforts to achieve a fair transition. Many people lack the resources to adapt to new, greener technologies, and the welfare state faces mounting pressures. In Central Europe, average income and purchasing power remain below the EU average. Old houses in small villages with low energy standards – and ageing, inefficient cars – render soon-to-be-implemented ETS2 legislation a potential time bomb for many.

The redistribution that once formed the basis of post-World War II prosperity in Europe now seems more like a utopia than an option. The narrative of 'fairness' or 'just transition' in European policies often focuses on compensating the most vulnerable, rather than engaging in the more difficult debate about wealth concentration and redistribution. Inequalities in bearing the costs of the transition exacerbate already pronounced disparities across European countries. Blaming climate change policies for social inequalities, unemployment, rising living costs, or decreasing purchasing power is far more convenient – especially in Central Europe – than addressing the roots of the problem, such as the diminishing power of the state vis-à-vis capital, flawed tax policies, or the privatisation of gains coupled with the socialisation of costs during the transition from post-centrally planned socialism.

In the wake of the Russian invasion of Ukraine and amid growing concerns about China, the European perception of a specific green social model is shifting – from promoting what could be to defending what already exists.

Unilateral steps toward true climate neutrality could, in practice (and at least in the short term), jeopardise the EU's position in the global economy. Geopolitics is rooted in power, and power depends on money and resources. While China declares its goal of climate neutrality by 2060, it carefully balances that target with its priority of economic growth. Russia outwardly expresses support for the transition but largely ignores the debate in practice. In the United States, the course shifted drastically after the 2024 elections, returning to a focus on fossil fuels and abandoning earlier commitments.

This is happening amid an increasingly unstable geopolitical landscape, with rising tensions and the threat of wars. The key question seems to be: How can we achieve climate neutrality within the framework of global competition for military, economic, and technological dominance while addressing internal tensions and keeping capitalism intact? At worst, it appears we may merely be pretending to believe in solutions to climate change. The political, regulatory, and financial frameworks being developed may simply test the limits of what is possible without clashing with powerful geopolitical and financial interests.

Time, inequality, and geopolitics define the manoeuvring space for Central Europe in this complex game, while the European Union itself plays an ambiguous role. Central European countries – including Poland, Hungary, Slovakia, and the Czech Republic – have long viewed the 'West' and the EU as models to emulate. EU accession provided them with a vision, benchmarks, and ambitions. After joining, these countries experienced significant GDP growth facilitated by access to a single market of over 450 million consumers, increased trade and investment, and substantial foreign direct investment in manufacturing, infrastructure, and technology sectors. These developments modernised industries and created jobs, alongside political and institutional benefits such as incentives for reform, improved governance, and enhanced transparency and efficiency.

Yet, two decades later, growing disillusionment has set in – partly fuelled by the region's emancipation and evolving identity. Central European governments often perceive EU rules and oversight – particularly in areas like the rule of law, judicial independence, and media freedom – as intrusions on national sovereignty. While EU membership allowed citizens to travel, work, and study freely, it also triggered a massive brain drain that exacerbated demographic decline. The imposition of migrant quotas was deeply unpopular and seen as the West offloading its problems onto the East.

After more than three decades of unification, many Central Europeans feel they are treated as second-class members of the EU. Coalition and opposition leaders in Hungary or Poland have leveraged Euroskeptic narratives to build domestic support, portraying the EU as an outsider imposing unwelcome rules. Similarly, in Slovakia, actions by the European Commission are often depicted as applying double standards, favouring certain political parties over others.

In this context, climate policy has become a battlefield, with the Green Deal serving as a symbol of perceived EU overreach and misunderstanding of local problems and conditions. This sentiment is not entirely unfounded. Transitioning to climate neutrality imposes economic and social costs that are often seen as disproportionately affecting less wealthy Central European countries. Dependence on Russian energy, coupled with EU pressure for a green transition, has created tensions as governments struggle to balance energy security with climate commitments. The result is that energy costs in Central and Eastern Europe (CEE) remain higher than in wealthier Western European countries, impacting both households and industries.

The problem with these arguments – sometimes data-driven but often skewed – is twofold. First, they downplay the scope and severity of climate change threats to the Central European region. More dangerously, in the short term, resistance to climate change policies is often used as a vehicle to promote outdated ideas from the 1990s: the illusion of unlimited markets, the portrayal of the welfare state as a burden on progress, and the characterisation of green activism as an internal enemy. It is within this context that Central European priorities must be critically discussed, and we must search for new visions.

4.2. We Are All Stakeholders Now

Central Europe faces a complex web of challenges in its transition toward climate neutrality. Since the fall of communism in 1989 and the subsequent integration of Central European countries into global capitalism – particularly through EU membership – the region has undergone profound economic and spatial restructuring. The shift from centrally planned to market economies opened the door for multinational corporations to invest in Central Europe. Countries such as Poland, the Czech Republic, Slovakia, and Hungary became attractive destinations for foreign direct investment. Joining the EU in 2004 further boosted investor confidence, attracting non-European capital seeking cost-effective access to the Single European Market. A typical example is the car manufacturing industry in Slovakia, where 1990s investments by Volkswagen were later followed by South Korean and Kia investments in the post-EU accession period.

Access to structural funds has enabled large-scale investments in infrastructure, further fuelling investment flows. Improved roads, railways, energy grids, and urban development projects have created new spaces for capital accumulation. As David Harvey (2010) describes, Central Europe has provided 'spatial fixes' for capitalism – a process in which capital moves to new geographical locations to overcome crises by opening up new markets and investment opportunities. These spatial fixes are often accompanied by 'temporal fixes', whereby crises are deferred into the future through credit and debt mechanisms. By creating new spaces for investment or extending credit, capitalism temporarily resolves its contradictions while laying the groundwork for future crises and potential backlash.

While Central Europe has benefitted from increased investment and development, these spatial fixes have also generated new contradictions, including rising inequality, environmental degradation, and growing social resistance. Investment has been heavily concentrated in major cities such as Warsaw, Prague, Budapest, and Bratislava, often leaving rural areas underdeveloped. This uneven development is a hallmark of spatial fixes, as capital gravitates toward areas with the highest potential returns. Moreover, Central Europe's economic model – relying heavily on FDI and EU funds – renders the region vulnerable to external shocks, a vulnerability particularly evident in industries like automotive manufacturing.

The transition to climate neutrality could represent a new spatial fix, with capital shifting toward green technologies. Yet, as discussed in this book, aside from some positive trends in Poland, this shift has not materialised strongly. The old model is under threat, and the new model is not yet robust enough. Consequently, the future of the European economic model remains uncertain, and anxiety is growing in Central Europe.

As Branko Milanović (2019) writes in *Capitalism, Alone*, the whole world has become an integral part of capitalism, and for the first time in human history, one economic system dominates the globe. We are all stakeholders now, dependent on our physical and social security, well-being, and prospects within this system. We face a growing metabolic rift and detachment from nature, while our social status and income depend on an ever-accelerating treadmill of production. Stability in capitalism is closely tied to economic growth, yet achieving carbon neutrality would require a fundamental belief that green growth can truly replace fossil-based growth – a perception that struggles to find solid ground in Central European politics.

Moreover, adverse effects on growth are compounded by prevailing pessimistic perspectives, which are deeply rooted in Central European cultural heritage and are increasingly common across the continent. The future of Europe's role in the global production and consumption system is uncertain. For the first time in history, investment flows are not only directed from North to South or West to East; China is now massively investing in Europe and challenging the technological edge of the continent.

Since the 1990s, mainstream narratives in Central Europe have been built around 'catching up' with the most developed Western countries or detaching from the past of centrally planned economies. This detachment was partially achieved by undermining the role of the state, welfare policies, and redistribution mechanisms, which in turn led to skyrocketing inequalities and an increasing concentration of capital. A small but growing elite in Central Europe has amassed considerable wealth, often linked to the privatisation processes of the 1990s. Although we are all stakeholders, power has become increasingly concentrated.

It is hardly surprising that capital in Central Europe now seeks 'temporal fixes' to counteract declining economic growth, searching for market expansion as a remedy for problems generated by a system that is increasingly running on borrowed time. This search manifests in the proliferation of leasing arrangements, consumer loans, and credit card debt. It is no longer enough for the well-off to buy things they do not need while those less fortunate cannot cover basic expenses; increasingly, people are financing their basic needs with money they do not have. During economic recessions, many find themselves unable to pay their debts, resulting in consumption levels that exceed rational limits and spirals that lead to bankruptcy. For instance, in the Czech Republic – a nation of 10 million in 2023 – 631,500 people, or more than 6% of the population, face enforcement proceedings initiated by creditors.

The metabolic rift between humanity and nature is not narrowing. On the contrary, as neoliberal policies deepen in Central Europe, our dependence on existing infrastructure is also increasing. If your retirement in Slovakia depends on privatised pension funds trading on volatile stock markets, your best interest is tied to continuous economic growth. Similarly, if your job in car manufacturing is threatened by emerging competition from China, protecting the market becomes a priority. In such an environment, manufacturing jobs are increasingly at risk, often replaced by lower-paid service sector positions. This paints a picture of a society that struggles to move forward and must expend significant energy and resources merely to maintain its current standard of living. We are all stakeholders, yet many fear losing what we already have.

Meanwhile, the system perpetuates the illusion that we are all in the same boat: shareholders, factory owners, and even the last employee on the assembly line. We all depend on the infrastructure of modern society and the need for access to increasingly privatised public goods. However, from a climate change perspective, the assembly line worker is more akin to a stoker on the Titanic – having little influence on the ship's course, not sharing in the wealth generated by fellow workers, and facing lower survival odds than first-class passengers in the short run.

The number of people who vocally support stronger measures to combat climate change varies dramatically among countries but is consistently lower in Central Europe compared to the rest of Europe. While one might blame deficiencies in education or media, a plausible explanation also lies in the vulnerability of those who feel threatened by a system with diminishing social protections and fear instability reminiscent of the 1990s.

Contradictory trends thus emerge in Central Europe. The more threatened people feel, the more they rally behind those offering solutions. Yet very often, those who demand job and physical security are the same individuals who undermine social security. When treated narrowly within the framework of ecological modernisation, climate change policies can become a lightning rod that distracts from the need for a complex approach to social and economic transformation – a transformation essential for addressing the climate threat without exacerbating inequalities and vulnerabilities, which could ultimately accelerate climate crises.

Only by broadening the focus from capitalism-centric growth to a society centred on human well-being within planetary limits can we begin to work toward real solutions. We are all system stakeholders now, and any challenge to the system may seem utopian. Although it is rare for a single stakeholder to dismantle or 'defeat' a system, history shows that individuals or groups driven by powerful ideas born of necessity can spark significant change and catalyse broader movements that challenge entrenched systemic structures.

The challenge may begin with three pillars: questioning the purported 'historical' logic of neoliberalism, redefining production and enhancing the self-sufficiency of the European industrial and economic model, and building a new vision of a welfare and ecological state.

4.3. Challenging Neoliberalisation

The collapse of centrally planned economies in Central and Eastern Europe occurred at a time when the Western economic model was increasingly under pressure to deregulate – and, paraphrasing Eric Hobsbawm (1994), the golden age of capitalism was over. The narratives and discourses of key actors, such as the World Bank, IMF, and European Commission, shaped policies that were inevitably reflected in the transformation process. Although competing visions existed on how to transition from planned socialism to market economies, all four countries ultimately embraced neoliberal reforms.

Neoliberalism is generally characterised by market-oriented policies aimed at deregulating capital markets, eliminating price controls, and reducing trade barriers. It emphasises privatisation, deregulation, and a shift toward individual responsibility, often reducing the role of the state in economic and social life. This process began under the influence and pressure of Western advisers and institutions but quickly found domestic support among emerging elites. Neoliberalism soon became the dominant ideology in Central Europe's political landscape, where the left was defeated and ostracised, the state was associated with past failures, and social protections or collective interests were framed as obstacles to growth and prosperity. These political trends were later supplanted in the 2000s by increasing nationalism and right-wing populism, which, however, rarely challenge the core economic tenets of neoliberalism.

Decarbonisation as a state-led project, however, clashes with the broader context of the neoliberal state, which has become the prevailing political arrangement. On one hand, neoliberal tendencies emphasise minimising state influence in the economy through privatisation and deregulation – or, as Cerny and Evans (2001) argue, by disempowering the state from within, reducing its role in key tasks and activities. On the other hand, decarbonisation requires a top-down approach involving the planning and implementation of central policies and measures.

These contradictions create structural obstacles embedded in the current political setup. Governments face pressure from businesses operating in the global and Single European Market to reduce regulations, privatise public assets, and limit state intervention, even as countries confront increasing social costs of decarbonisation and pressure on the state budget – partly mitigated by European Structural and Cohesion Funds.

Although Central European countries as of 2025 are either below the EU average in debt levels (e.g. Slovakia, Poland, and the Czech Republic) or only slightly above (Hungary), they are burdened by significant dividend outflows, low wages combined with ineffective taxation, and rising economic and social costs. These pressures further drive austerity measures, public spending cuts, deregulation, and laissez-faire expansion.

The success of the transition to climate neutrality depends on many external and internal factors, but primarily on the ability of states to challenge neoliberal tendencies that undermine transformation at multiple levels. Many companies profit from the weak internalisation of external social costs into product prices, while states increasingly struggle to finance education, research and development, infrastructure, and healthcare. Analysing the emergence of a low-carbon policy framework as an ideological state-level project (Wei 2021) reveals that steering economic transformation requires significant investment – investments that are constrained by the neoliberal system. Decarbonisation policies and neoliberalisation are inherently in tension because they arise from different goals and frameworks, addressing the roles of the state, market, and social priorities in fundamentally opposing ways.

The challenge lies in focusing on structural issues rather than merely treating symptoms. Central Europe's reliance on coal and other fossil fuels is a legacy of historical economic structures. Neoliberal policies slow the phase-out of these industries by prioritising market-driven transitions over planned interventions. Large-scale investments in renewable energy, energy efficiency, public transportation, and green technologies are crucial – yet markets alone are unlikely to provide sufficient funding.

In its current form, climate neutrality is largely a project of ecological modernisation. Central European countries must significantly transform their economic and social systems by downsizing fossil fuel-based industries and transitioning to decarbonised production and consumption patterns. Even at this non-systemic level, such 'creative destruction' is difficult to achieve without targeted state interventions, coordinated regional governance, efforts to redirect private investments, and active policies that harness market forces and mobilise stakeholders.

Achieving climate neutrality goals will therefore require rethinking the neoliberal paradigm, particularly in terms of equity, social intervention, regulation, and increased state engagement. For Central Europe, transitioning beyond neoliberal frameworks is essential. Countries must adopt models that prioritise public investment, state-led planning, and collective action – concepts long dismissed as relics of the past. Rejecting the constraints of neoliberalism would allow Central Europe to build a more equitable and sustainable future while meeting its climate goals.

The most pressing challenge is social. As Bob Jessop (2023) highlights, the post-World War II emphasis on Keynesian policies to address market imperfections has been replaced by a neoliberal perspective grounded in a Schumpeterian workfare state. This shift prioritises globalisation, economic competitiveness, and workforce participation over traditional welfare provisioning. Fair and equitable policies that distribute the costs of the green transition justly are essential to prevent public backlash.

However, three decades of neoliberal capitalism in Central Europe have exacerbated income and wealth disparities – benefiting elites while marginalising low-income groups. Market deregulation has led to insecure jobs, low wages, and weakened worker protections. The privatisation of services, re-commodification of labour, and outsourcing of production have systematically undermined what remains of the welfare state.

We do not need to start with revolution, but with relatively simple steps. Economic and social cohesion is critical for managing the risks associated with decarbonisation. The 'elephant in the room' is the need for an open debate on reassessing the tax system. Addressing the costs of the transition and achieving the 2050 climate neutrality goals will likely require a combination of progressive taxation and eco-social tax reform to redistribute the costs of decarbonisation more evenly. Current trends, however, suggest further deterioration of social and human rights, with an overemphasis on economic growth at the expense of broader social and environmental goals like equity and sustainability.

In the 2023 general elections in Slovakia and the 2024 EU parliamentary elections in the Czech Republic, populist parties campaigned on protecting the combustion engine against expensive and 'nonsense' electric cars – issues that helped propel these politicians into parliament. The relatively negative perception of climate policies or the Green Deal in Central Europe can, to some extent, be attributed to local political struggles in which decarbonisation is often blamed for unemployment or rising living costs, while deeper structural causes – such as weak state capacity, inadequate taxation, or privatisation – are deliberately overlooked.

Within this framework, the European Union's approach to the green transformation and its commitment to a 'Just Transition' can be seen as an end-of-the-pipe solution – an attempt to redistribute burdens rather than fundamentally altering the dynamics of wealth concentration and co-opting powerful business and industrial interests. To be serious about climate neutrality requires systemic approaches (e.g. rethinking the welfare state) rather than piecemeal solutions (e.g. energy poverty bonuses or temporary compensations).

Addressing the structural, social, and financial barriers necessary to confront the climate crisis requires robust public support and an empowered civil society. Confronting the inherent tensions between profit-driven motives and the social equity goals essential for the transition demands a broadly shared vision of a climate-neutral future. In its absence, decarbonisation may simply amount to greening the existing system – providing a measure of stability while the promise of a fully decarbonised future remains mired in uncertainties and risks.

4.4. Strategic Low-Carbon Autonomy

In an increasingly polarised world where Europe is gradually losing its traditional competitive advantages, the continent faces a choice: continue struggling to maintain its position or acknowledge the need for a fundamentally different strategy. As many historical analyses have shown, the core of the global economy has fluctuated between East and West – shifting from the Venetian Republic to the Dutch provinces, from the United Kingdom to the United States – while its current trajectory inevitably points towards Asia. The typical response of core countries losing their influence has often been military, but wars have never succeeded in altering what is essentially a mixture of structural conditions, demographic shifts, and internal economic dynamics.

The EU's current strategy to respond to geopolitical challenges and global competition focuses on boosting competitiveness, reflecting calls for deregulation, and dismantling social protections viewed as obstacles to keeping pace with future global leaders. While this approach may yield temporary results, it risks merely delaying the inevitable, placing the burden of unsustainable growth on future generations.

A point of departure for alternative thinking may lie in further developing the concept of strategic autonomy – more specifically, strategic low-carbon autonomy. While the concept of strategic autonomy is not new, it has traditionally focused on protecting and promoting domestic production of key goods and commodities while deepening the common European market. The primary justification has been safeguarding technologies and entire production chains to ensure that the EU remains in control and at the forefront of strategic technological and industrial development.

In a broader sense, strategic autonomy involves redefining the future of Europe's industrial base and harnessing its potential to create new labour opportunities. The rationale is to level the playing field with key global competitors, particularly China, which is often criticised for providing direct and indirect subsidies and employing unfair practices in its production chains, leading to unbalanced competition. By fostering self-reliance in critical industries, the EU can shield itself from external shocks and secure a competitive edge in emerging markets, especially those tied to the green economy.

The roots of strategic autonomy can be traced back to the 1990s, particularly with the establishment of the Common Foreign and Security Policy under the Maastricht Treaty (1992) and the subsequent creation of the European Security and Defence Policy in the late 1990s. These efforts aimed to make the EU more responsible for its own security and defence matters, especially after the Balkan conflicts exposed its reliance on NATO (and, by extension, the United States) for military interventions.

The term 'strategic autonomy' gained renewed emphasis with the adoption of the EU Global Strategy (EUGS) in 2016. Spearheaded by then-High Representative Federica Mogherini, the strategy explicitly called for greater EU autonomy in external actions, emphasising stronger European defence capabilities and a more assertive global role. However, the concept expanded significantly in the following years to encompass economic priorities alongside defence, driven by global events such as the 2008 financial crisis, growing competition and trade tensions with the United States, the COVID-19 pandemic, and the Russian-Ukrainian war in 2022. These events underscored the EU's vulnerabilities and justified the push for greater self-reliance.

The COVID-19 pandemic highlighted the EU's overreliance on global supply chains for critical goods such as medical supplies, pharmaceuticals, and semiconductors, accelerating the push for strategic autonomy in economic and industrial policies. Similarly, geopolitical tensions, particularly with Russia, prompted efforts to diversify energy sources, invest in renewable energy, and reduce dependence on Russian oil and gas. This shift has not only redefined the EU's energy policies but also amplified the urgency of transitioning to sustainable energy systems to secure long-term resilience.

Building on these recent experiences and the changing geopolitical division between core and periphery, it is time to consider how to further develop the autonomy concept. Strategic low-carbon autonomy presents an opportunity to secure a resilient, socially stabilised Europe – an economic model for the future, where advanced climate change transformation, now seen by many as a luxury, becomes a necessity.

This autonomy must begin with energy. Coal, gas, and oil need to be replaced by a combination of nuclear energy, providing baseload stability, and renewable sources like wind and solar. These investments serve a dual purpose: reducing dependence on imported fossil fuels and enhancing energy security while minimising vulnerability to energy price fluctuations. Simultaneously, energy efficiency measures targeting industry, transport, and households can reduce economic and social risks while fostering domestic innovation and stimulating the development of green technologies.

Food security represents another critical pillar of the strategic autonomy debate, reflecting both immediate and long-term challenges posed by climate change, shifting geopolitical dynamics, and vulnerabilities in international supply chains. Climate trends, including rising temperatures, altered precipitation patterns, and increased frequency of extreme weather events, will disrupt agricultural production globally. The EU must integrate eco-agricultural goals with production objectives, balancing environmental sustainability with the need to secure reliable food supplies.

Strategic autonomy is further justified by the need to manage the EU's decarbonisation process while protecting domestic industries from the associated costs and the unfair competitive advantages enjoyed by countries with lower environmental and social standards. By internalising these costs, the EU can support the maintenance and transformation of its industrial base. Industries face intense competition within the single market and must accelerate their transition to remain competitive, but strategic autonomy can shield them from external pressures. Many voices within the business community argue that without systematic protection and support for decarbonising production, entire segments of Europe's heavy industry risk extinction.

Critically viewed, strategic autonomy represents an effort to reverse some of the effects of globalisation, which no longer favours the EU as it once did. While the outsourcing of production and the shift from manufacturing to service economies – a hallmark of the 1970s neoliberal reforms – initially benefitted Europe, these trends now threaten to reduce the EU to a consumer economy, increasingly dependent on other continents for both raw materials and finished goods.

Increasing the EU's capacity to act independently in economic, defence, technological, and foreign policy domains without over-reliance on external powers like the United States or China offers potential benefits. However, achieving strategic autonomy would require a long-term political vision that unites member states and political factions around the principles of green industrial transformation. This is particularly challenging given the increasing concentration of manufacturing in Central European countries like Poland, the Czech Republic, and Slovakia, alongside traditional industrial hubs in Germany, Sweden, and Austria.

A comparison between Luxembourg and Poland illustrates the challenges ahead. Since the 1970s, deindustrialisation has transformed Luxembourg's economy from an industrial powerhouse to a service-oriented hub. In contrast, Poland experienced a significant revival of manufacturing after joining the EU in 2004, developing a renewed industrial base focused on heavy industry, metallurgy, and automotive production.

The automotive industry epitomises the challenges of the green transition. Despite temporary slowdowns, the shift toward electrification and new powertrains is inevitable. This transition presents risks for Europe, particularly for car-producing nations, but strategic plans from leading countries and automotive manufacturers indicate that it is non-negotiable. The EU will need to double down on the transformation, supporting it politically and through policies and measures that encourage battery research and production, decarbonise supply chains, and assist small and medium-sized enterprises in adapting to the new industrial landscape.

Defining industrial support under the framework of strategic low-carbon autonomy requires coordinated action while adhering to the principles of the Single European Market. Environmental and climate objectives are central to justifying this approach. The argument is that retaining control over industrial production within the EU, where stricter environmental standards apply, is preferable to relying on imports from countries with lower environmental standards and unaccounted-for carbon costs.

Pursuing strategic low-carbon autonomy carries risks of counter-reactions, isolationism, stagnation, and even new trade wars with unpredictable outcomes. It may have environmental and social impacts both internally and externally. It therefore requires careful cost-benefit analyses and broad discussion within the EU and with global partners.

A good example is the Carbon Border Adjustment Mechanism (CBAM), designed to level the playing field for EU industries by imposing carbon costs on imports from countries without equivalent carbon pricing. Strengthening and enforcing this mechanism is crucial for maintaining the competitiveness of European industries, such as steel, within the single market. However, CBAM may provoke retaliatory measures from trading partners, sparking new trade disputes and further complicating international relations.

Europe's engagement with strategic autonomy raises many questions about the future of global trade. The EU must decide whether it wants to retain its manufacturing base and, if so, develop a robust green industrial policy to attract investments, accelerate development, and drive the transition to a low-carbon economy. Currently, the EU lacks a cohesive industrial policy. While platforms for European strategic technologies and projects of common European interest exist, they remain fragmented and lack an overarching vision. Addressing this gap will require embedding competitiveness, security, and fairness principles into a coherent strategic autonomy framework.

Further progress towards autonomy may have significant environmental impacts. Reindustrialisation will inevitably increase pressure on resources, waste management, and pollution. Efforts to ensure food security could exacerbate biodiversity loss, increase pressure to expand arable land, and amplify pesticide pollution. Current criticism of environmental and climate legislation and calls for deregulation may further endanger the already fragile state of the European environment. The concept of low-carbon strategic autonomy needs to develop hand in hand with increased environmental and climate protection, not in antagonism or conflict.

Reshoring production and supply chains may offer a clearer picture of the true ecological footprint of the continent, potentially driving more transparent and accountable environmental and climate policies. While strategic low-carbon autonomy offers a pathway to strengthen Europe's economic and industrial resilience, it must be pursued with careful consideration of its broader economic, geopolitical, and environmental implications. The success will depend on the EU's ability to balance competitiveness, sustainability, and global cooperation in an increasingly complex and interconnected world.

4.5. From Welfare State to Eco-State?

Strategic low-carbon autonomy, combined with addressing neoliberalisation trends, may provide solid ground for a future European economic model with better chances to adapt to climate change. Yet, confronting the prevailing narratives of deregulated capitalism – albeit with a green image – requires a broadly shared, publicly supported vision of a climate-neutral future. Otherwise, we risk alternative scenarios.

Based on his analysis of pre–World War II developments, Karl Polanyi (1944) argued that the tendency to release the economy from social control inevitably provokes a counter-movement – a defensive reaction. However, history has shown that society's defensive responses do not necessarily lead to more democratic or equitable solutions; they may instead introduce new forms of control that curtail human rights in the name of 'stability'.

The possibility of different reactions and counter-reactions raises several urgent questions: What alternative vision of the future should Central Europe develop to address climate challenges? How can current tendencies and threats be counterbalanced? For instance, is the region on an irreversible trajectory toward embracing Viktor Orbán's concept of 'illiberal democracy'? Or, as Branko Milanović asks, what prospects exist for a fairer world in an era when capitalism seems to be the 'only game in town'?

If we agree on the need for deep systemic change – beyond surface-level fixes – to achieve genuine justice and equity rather than perpetuating existing inequalities, then decarbonisation must be seen as more than a cosmetic adjustment. Instead, it should be regarded as an opportunity to fundamentally redefine state functions and goals. The intersection of social and environmental objectives offers a framework for rethinking the state's role in addressing both old and new challenges. We may explore these possibilities by rethinking the success of the European welfare state and by conceptualising and discussing the idea of an eco-state.

James Meadowcroft describes the eco-state as one that places ecological concerns at the centre of its governance, much like the welfare state regulates the effects of the market (Meadowcroft 2005:3). Similarly, the term 'eco-state', as understood by Lafferty (1998), refers to a political unit that integrates ecological principles into its constitution and governance. Scholars such as Robyn Eckersley argue that the eco-state aligns with green political theory by prioritising ecological well-being and intergenerational justice. However, many interpretations stop short of fully intertwining environmental goals with social security, often focusing instead on mechanisms and policies inspired by the welfare state.

In our view, the eco-state must go deeper. It should represent a governance model that integrates ecological sustainability into the core functions of the state while emphasising equity, social security, and intergenerational justice. It should address inequalities by redistributing profits and compensating for externalities – both social and environmental – that are not accounted for in the direct costs of generating profit.

To explore where environmental protection, ecological limits, and welfare systems intersect, we can begin with several key assumptions grounded in historical experience and empirical evidence. First, reducing social inequalities positively influences the creation and implementation of environmental policies. Contrary to the notion that higher social protection depends on environmentally harmful mass consumption, quality of life and social security can be achieved without perpetuating resource-intensive production and consumption systems. Combining an environmental vision with a social alternative focused on addressing inequality may generate broader support for systemic changes.

The relationship between social inequality and environmental harm operates on multiple levels. For example, James K. Boyce's research in the United States shows that states with greater social inequality – such as Tennessee, Alabama, and Mississippi – experience higher pollution levels and have weaker environmental laws than more equitable states like Minnesota, Maine, and Wisconsin (Boyce 2002; Boyce et al. 2006). In Europe, similar historical contrasts can be drawn between Scandinavian countries and, for instance, Great Britain.

Social inequality exacerbates environmental risks and unevenly distributes their impacts. Low-income or marginalised groups are often disproportionately exposed to environmental hazards, leading to spatial segregation, social exclusion, and unequal access to decision-making processes. Polarised societies tend to invest fewer resources in addressing environmental and social challenges, thereby deepening these inequalities.

In contrast, an eco-state would recognise that social protection and quality of life need not depend on environmentally harmful mass consumption. This counters the argument that welfare state redistribution inherently stimulates unsustainable consumption. Instead, the eco-state must redefine economic and social goals, moving beyond the dominant paradigm of growth-driven production and consumption.

Reassessing consumption and production goals is the first step. As Gabor Steingart (2008) observed, people do not simply desire cheap consumer goods – they also value job security and access to quality public services. This raises the question: Would most people prefer disposable income for direct consumption, or better access to healthcare, education, and safety nets in times of need? The eco-state must offer a vision of reduced resource-intensive consumption while enhancing opportunities for self-realisation and mitigating social and environmental risks.

What is ecologically harmful (e.g. fossil fuels, private car use) should be expensive, while what is socially beneficial (e.g. healthcare, education, culture) should be affordable and accessible. Achieving this requires not only ecological tax reform but a complete rethinking of the goals of production and consumption.

Generating public support for the eco-state is a crucial starting point. Environmental problems, unlike the immediate threats addressed by the welfare state, often fail to generate broad societal consensus. As we have discussed in relation to the concept of the *Metabolic Rift*, public support typically arises in response to specific, localised crises rather than a recognition of systemic issues. To build support for the eco-state, it is essential to raise awareness of environmental risks and frame climate action as delivering tangible social and economic benefits.

James Meadowcroft's analysis of the welfare state's development provides valuable lessons for the eco-state. Both models require state authority, an alternative to market-based solutions, and continuous adaptation to economic, social, and environmental changes (Meadowcroft 2005:11). Importantly, the welfare state achieved mass support by addressing immediate social needs and threats. Similarly, the eco-state must demonstrate concrete benefits for the middle and working classes to gain legitimacy and sustain its political base.

For many in Central Europe, climate change is perceived as a threat rather than an opportunity. The idea of an eco-state may, therefore, seem utopian. There are many open questions, and at present, we are still in the stage of protecting the remnants of the welfare state, not yet considering its expansion. Yet, an economy increasingly released from social control already provokes counter-movements and defensive reactions in which climate and environmental goals become collateral damage.

If we are to confront illiberal tendencies combined with the exploitation of the planet beyond climate tipping points, we need to build new alternatives – and the concept of an eco-state may be a step in the right direction. As Murray Bookchin (1987) pointed out, utopian ideas serve as mirrors to current society, offering transformative visions based on new values. While scepticism about alternatives is understandable, ignoring them only perpetuates the status quo. Public discourse must engage with such alternatives, even amid the inertia of entrenched capitalist systems.

Contrary to mainstream perspectives, the task is no longer about saving the current neoliberal model. Any viable alternative – whether labelled as an eco-state or otherwise – must respect ecological limits, redefine growth, and emphasise social and environmental justice. Just as the welfare state emerged from economic crises and complex negotiations among capital, politics, and society, the eco-state will face similar obstacles. Whether and when such a transformation can occur without a deep climate crisis remains an open question.

Between a Rock and a Hard Place

A popular illusion in recent Central European public discourse is the notion of a 'decaying West' – eroded by decades of welfare policies and utopian green targets – juxtaposed with an 'agile East', supposedly freed from the shackles of centrally planned socialism only to be hindered by unwise and unrealistic EU policies.

In reality, what we more likely see is a confused East, unsure of which vision to pursue. Central Europe's perspective on climate change – and, more broadly, on future development – reflects its historical and sensitive position as part of the semi-periphery within the broader European and global context. Historically, Central Europe has functioned as a transitional space – economically, politically, and socially – between the wealthier, industrially advanced 'core' countries of Western Europe and the less developed economies of Eastern Europe.

Revisiting Immanuel Wallerstein (2005), the region's trajectory does not suggest that it will soon reach the living standards or cultural-institutional levels of the most developed European countries. While economic progress has been made – particularly in Poland, which aspires to regional economic prominence – the path from semi-periphery to core status remains fraught with challenges. This status is deeply rooted in history, and one could argue that Central Europe, both before WWII and after the political changes of the 1990s, has experienced various forms of neocolonialism. For instance, Ivan Kalmar (2022) argues that dismissive attitudes toward 'Eastern Europeans' reflect a form of racism, where people from the region are seen as 'white but not quite' by their Western counterparts.

The political transformations following the collapse of centrally planned socialism were driven largely by a vision of joining the European core and overcoming such prejudices. However, the image of a stable and dominant 'West' – once seen as a model to emulate – is increasingly being questioned. The traditional core of the European economy now faces profound disruptions, including economic stagnation, political fragmentation, and widening social inequalities.

This raises questions about what constitutes the 'core' today, what it will look like in the future, and whether it remains a vision worth pursuing. The official slogan of our times may be 'competitiveness', but the underlying narrative is one of economic – and potentially military – confrontation. The West's declining geopolitical position, coupled with shifting production and consumption patterns and the system's inability to generate sufficient resources to maintain its dominance, risks rendering climate policies collateral damage in a race to the bottom.

The brutal neoliberalisation and dismantling of social rights once touted as a miraculous cure for Central Europe's development gap have, three decades later, revealed their limitations. Although relative economic progress has been achieved, it has come at the expense of eroding social foundations, facilitating capital outflows, weakening educational and healthcare systems, and creating widespread social insecurity – even among the middle class. This context helps explain Central Europe's flirtation with illiberalism, calls for 'traditional values', and a longing for stability – trends not unlike those seen in many Western countries.

The challenges facing Europe are compounded by geopolitical shifts and technological transformations, which threaten the long-standing structures of power and prosperity within the core while leaving the semi-periphery in an uncertain position. For Central Europe, this dynamic creates a dual challenge. On one hand, the region seeks to advance its economic and social standing by aligning with the core through innovation, industrial modernisation, and EU integration. On the other hand, it must navigate the vulnerabilities of a crumbling core that no longer guarantees stability, cohesion, or equitable development opportunities.

Two negative political narratives have recently emerged in Central Europe in response to the Green Deal and its anticipated economic and social implications – both of which downplay the urgency and impacts of climate change.

The first narrative claims that climate concerns are temporary distractions and that the EU has been 'hijacked' by green idealists and weak politicians. In this view, the solution is to return to a pre–Green Deal era of deregulation, market freedom, and competitiveness – a narrative that gained further traction in Europe following the 2025 US policy shift toward climate change denial.

The second framework assumes that Europe is in decline and that successful countries must adopt a more independent stance, leveraging their semi-peripheral status to position themselves between the West and the emerging East. Poland and the Czech Republic often embody the first perspective, while Hungary and Slovakia lean toward the second, attempting to attract investments from the East and emancipate themselves from mainstream EU policies.

Regardless of these perspectives, the region's heavy reliance on industries and energy systems rooted in high-carbon, resource-intensive models – combined with a shared belief in the neoliberal development paradigm – shapes negative attitudes toward climate policies. Structural conditions such as limited resources, weaker institutional capacities, and reliance on outdated economic models further complicate efforts to meet ambitious EU climate targets.

Currently, very few political parties or movements openly support the Green Deal and the 2050 climate neutrality target. When support does exist, it typically comes from opposition benches in parliament. Mainstream politics in all four Central European countries seriously entertains the option that the EU might eventually abandon the Green Deal altogether; if not entirely, then climate policies may become irrelevant as the EU prioritises economic growth over climate concerns.

Geopolitically, Central Europe may be likened to the tail of a dog – it cannot wag the dog but is inevitably wagged by it. Yet, the power of smaller regions and countries lies in their ability to unite. Climate change is an existential threat that demands collective action, and Central Europe has opportunities to shape the global and European climate agenda. The region's history of rapid structural change – from centrally planned economies to market-driven systems – offers valuable lessons for navigating transitions. Its strong industrial base and strategic geographic location position it as a potential hub for green innovation, regional cooperation, and a bridge between global players.

However, Central Europe also faces existential questions: How can it leverage its semi-peripheral position to drive sustainable and equitable development? How can it adapt to the uncertainties of a shifting global and European order while avoiding past mistakes? And how can it ensure that its transition contributes to rebuilding resilient and inclusive societies rather than perpetuating inequality and fragmentation? Climate change forces us to rethink sustainability, shifting the focus from the quantity of macroeconomic growth to the quality of development.

The essential question remains: Is capitalism a means or an end? For some, it is a tool for economic progress that must be harnessed and regulated; for others, it is a weapon for generating resources and achieving geopolitical dominance. Climate change presents both a mortal danger and an opportunity to rethink the global order. Achieving global climate neutrality requires moving from confrontation to cooperation, with systemic transformations across economic, political, social, and environmental dimensions.

As discussed throughout this book, the inherent logic of capitalism inevitably leads to environmental destruction. When the system works for sustainability, it does so only under societal pressure and strict regulatory constraints. Ecological modernisation and efforts to green capitalism in Central Europe have yielded some progress but are constrained by systemic limits. This is further compounded by weak states and civil societies – outcomes of drastic neoliberal reforms that discredited the old while failing to build a genuinely inclusive and sustainable new order.

Any meaningful climate discussion must begin by questioning the gradual neoliberalisation of the state in service of capital and envisioning viable alternatives to the current system. The economic and social transformations initiated in Central Europe in the early 1990s were guided by principles of state deconstruction. The result has been rising inequality, social insecurity, and weakened civil societies. In response to present and emerging challenges, Central European elites have largely doubled down on this path by advocating deregulation, securitisation, and the erosion of climate targets, social rights, and public welfare.

A recurring question in this book – perhaps idealistic – is this: Is it possible, and at what cost, to shift away from a system based on competition, overproduction, and overconsumption toward one grounded in sustainability and capable of addressing climate change? Can we create a system that provides jobs and opportunities for self-fulfilment without causing environmental destruction? Can we develop a framework that merges the achievements of the European welfare state with the principles of an eco-state – one where high-quality public services like education, transportation, and healthcare eliminate the need for private alternatives that exacerbate inequalities and strain natural resources? Or is the more realistic scenario one of growing inequalities, insecurity, and a relentless march toward climate catastrophe?

Bibliography

Andonova, L. (2004). *Transnational politics of the environment: The European Union and environmental policy in Central and Eastern Europe*. MIT Press.

Andonova, L., Mansfield, E. D., & Milner, H. V. (2007). International trade and environmental policy in the postcommunist world. *Comparative Political Studies, 40*(7), 782–807.

Angel, N. (1909). *The great illusion*. Simpkin, Marshall, Hamilton, Kent & Co. Retrieved from <https://archive.org/details/europesopticalil00angeuoft/page/n7/mode/2up?view=theater>

Arrighi, G. (1994). *The long twentieth century: Money, power and the origins of our times*. Verso.

Arrighi, G. (2000). Globalization and historical macrosociology. In J. Abu-Lughod (Ed.), *Sociology for the twenty-first century: Continuities and cutting edges* (pp. 145–160). University of Chicago Press.

Auer, M. R. (2004). *Restoring cursed earth: Appraising environmental policy reforms in Eastern Europe and Russia*. Rowman & Littlefield.

Barbosa, L. C. (2009). Theories in environmental sociology. In K. A. Gould & T. L. Lewis (Eds.), *Twenty lessons in environmental sociology* (pp. 57–73). Oxford University Press.

Barnes, P., & Barnes, I. (1999). *Environmental policy in the European Union*. Edward Elgar Publishing.

Beck, U. (1999). *World risk society*. Polity Press.

Bell, M. L., Davis, D. L., & Fletcher, T. (2004). A retrospective assessment of mortality from the London smog episode of 1952: The role of influenza and pollution. *Environmental Health Perspectives, 112*(1), 6–9.

Bloomberg (BNEF). (2024). *New Energy Outlook 2024*. Retrieved from <https://about.bnef.com/new-energy-outlook/>

Bookchin, M. (1962). *Our synthetic environment*. Martino Fine Books.

Bookchin, M. (1987). Social ecology versus deep ecology: A challenge for the ecology movement. *Green Perspectives: Newsletter of the Green Program Project, 4–5* (Summer 1987). Retrieved 23 November 2010, from <http://www.ecology.gen.tr/deep-ecology/64-social-ecology-versus-deep-ecology.pdf>

Boyce, J. K. (2002). *The political economy of the environment*. Edward Elgar Publishing.

Boyce, J. K., Stanton, E., & Narain, S. (2006). *Reclaiming nature: Environmental justice and ecological restoration*. Anthem Press.

Braudel, F. (1993). *A history of civilization*. Penguin.

Brown, H., Derr, P., Renn, O., & White, A. (1993). *Corporate environmentalisms in the global economy*. Quorum Books.

Buttel, F. H. (2000). Ecological modernization as social theory. *Geoforum, 31*, 57–65.

Buttel, F. H. (2003). The treadmill of production: An appreciation, assessment, and agenda for research. [Lecture, Environment and Treadmill of Production symposium, University of Wisconsin]. Retrieved 4 June 2010, from <http://www.michaelmbell.net/RC24/papers/buttel.pdf>

Catton, W. (1982). Overshoot: The ecological basis of revolutionary change. Illini Books.

Catton, W., & Dunlap, R. E. (1978). Environmental sociology: A new paradigm. *American Sociologist, 13*, 41–49.

Cemy, P., & Evans, M. (2001). *New Labour, globalization, and the competition state* (Working Paper Series No. 70). Center for European Studies.

Clark, B., & Foster, B. (2001). William Stanley Jevons and the coal question: An introduction to Jevons' 'Of the economy of fuel'. *Organization & Environment, 14*(1), 93–98.

Department of Economic and Social Affairs of the United Nations Secretariat (UNDESA). (2009). *International Migration Report 2009: A Global Assessment*. Retrieved from <https://www.un.org/en/development/desa/population/migration/publications/migrationreport/docs/MigrationReport2009.pdf>

Dobson, A. (2000). *Green political thoughts.* Routledge.

Eckersley, R. (2004). *The green state: Rethinking democracy and sovereignty.* MIT Press.

Elkington, J. (1998). *Cannibals with forks: The triple bottom line of 21st-century business.* New Society Publisher.

Engels, F. (1969). *The condition of the working class in England, 1845.* Panther Edition.

European Central Bank. (2022). Fiscal policies to mitigate climate change in the euro area. *Economic Bulletin, (6).*

European Central Bank. (2024). Longer-term challenges for fiscal policy in the euro area. *ECB Economic Bulletin, 4/2024.* Retrieved from <https://www.ecb.europa.eu/press/economic-bulletin/articles/2024/html/ecb.ebart202404_02~d8159a215d.en.html>

European Commission. (2009). *Facing the future: Time for the EU to meet global challenges.* JRC-IPTS.

European Commission. (2010). *Europe 2020: Background information for the informal European Council, 11.2.2010.*

European Commission. (2010a). *Europe 2020: A strategy for smart, sustainable, and inclusive growth* (COM(2010) 3 March 2010). Brussels.

European Commission. (2013). *Commission staff working document: Adapting infrastructure to climate change.* Brussels.

European Commission. (2024). *The future of European competitiveness: A competitiveness strategy for Europe.*

European Commission. (2025). *A Competitiveness Compass for the EU* (COM(2025) 30 final). Brussels, 29 January 2025.

European Court of Auditors. (2023). *Special report: EU climate and energy targets 2020 targets achieved, but little indication that actions to reach the 2030 targets will be sufficient.* ECA.

European Environment Agency. (2007). *Europe's environment: The fourth assessment.* EEA.

European Environment Agency. (2010). *The European environment – state and outlook 2010: Synthesis.* EEA.

European Environment Agency. (2016). *Europe's environment: The Dobris Assessment – An overview of problems.* Retrieved from <https://www.eea.europa.eu/publications/92-827-5122-8/page014.html>

European Environment Agency. (2024). *The first European Climate Risk Assessment*. Retrieved from <https://www.cca.curopa.cu/publications/european-climate-risk-assessment>

European Environment Agency. (2024a). *Europe sustainability transition outlook*. Retrieved from <https://www.eea.europa.eu/publications/europes-sustainability-transitions-outlook>

Forzieri, G., et al. (2018). Escalating impacts of climate extremes on critical infrastructures in Europe. *Global Environmental Change, 48*, 97–107. <https://doi.org/10.1016/j.gloenvcha.2017.11.007>

Foster, J. B. (2002). *Ecology against capitalism*. Monthly Review Press.

Foster, J. B. (2009). *The ecological revolution: Making peace with the planet*. Monthly Review Press.

Foster, J. B. (2010). Capitalism and degrowth: An impossibility theorem. *Monthly Review, 62*(8). Retrieved 10 February 2011, from <http://www.monthlyreview.org/110101foster.php>

Gerschenkron, A. (1962). *Economic backwardness in historical perspective: A book of essays*. The Belknap Press.

Giddens, A. (2009). *Politics of climate change*. Polity Press.

Gonzalez, G. A. (2001). Democratic ethics and ecological modernization: The formulation of California's automobile emission standards. *Public Integrity, 3*, 325–344.

Gould, K. A., Pellow, D. N., & Schnaiberg, A. (2004). Interrogating the treadmill of production: Everything you wanted to know about the treadmill but were afraid to ask. *Organization & Environment, 17*, 296–316.

Graham, E., & Fulghum, N. (2024). Wind and solar overtake EU fossil fuels in the first half of 2024. Retrieved from <https://ember-energy.org/latest-insights/eu-wind-and-solar-overtake-fossil-fuels/>

Gramsci, A. (1971). *Selections from the prison notebooks* (Q. Hoare & G. N. Smith, Eds. & Trans.). International Publishers. (Original work published 1971)

Gray, J. (2009). Gray's Anatomy: John Gray's Selected Writings. Allen Lane.

Groys, B. (2010, 1 March). Revoluce ctnosti – Na sociálním státu vydělávají převážně bohatí. *Babylon*.

Hajer, M. A. (1995). *The politics of environmental discourse: Ecological modernization and the policy process*. Oxford University Press.

Harman, C. (2008). *A people's history of the world*. Verso.

Harvey, D. (2010). *The enigma of capital and the crises of capitalism*. Profile Books.

Harvey, D. (2018). *A companion to Marx's Capital: The complete edition*. Verso Books.

Harvey, D. (2019). *Marx, Capital and the madness of economic reason*. Profile Books.

Havel, V. (1989). *Public speech, Prague, Czechoslovakia, December 1989*. Retrieved from <https://www.vaclavhavel.cz/cs/vaclav-havel/dilo/projevy>

Hawken, P., Lovins, A. B., & Lovins, L. H. (1999). *Natural capitalism: The next industrial revolution*. Earthscan.

High, S. A., & Lewis, D. W. (2007). *Corporate wasteland: The landscape and memory of deindustrialization*. Cornell University Press.

Hirsch, F. (1977). *Social limits to growth*. Routledge.

Hobsbawm, E. J. (1994). *The age of extremes: The short twentieth century, 1914–1991*. Michael Joseph.

Hobsbawm, E. J. (1999). *Industry and empire*. Penguin Books.

Horizon Databook. (2025). *The world's largest portal for market reports & statistics*. Retrieved from <https://www.grandviewresearch.com/>

Institute for Economics and Peace. (2020). *Over one billion people at threat of being displaced by 2050 due to environmental change, conflict, and civil unrest*. Retrieved from <https://www.economicsandpeace.org/wp-content/uploads/2020/09/Ecological-Threat-Register-Press-Release-27.08-FINAL.pdf>

Intergovernmental Panel on Climate Change. (2007). *Climate change 2007: Impacts, adaptation, and vulnerability*. Retrieved from <https://www.ipcc.ch/site/assets/uploads/2018/03/ar4_wg2_full_report.pdf>

Intergovernmental Panel on Climate Change. (2011). *The IPCC special report on managing the risks of extreme events and disasters to advance climate change adaptation*. IPCC.

Intergovernmental Panel on Climate Change. (2019). *IPCC annual report 2019: Protecting the world's plant resources from pests*. Retrieved from <https://www.ipcc.ch/>

Intergovernmental Panel on Climate Change. (2021). *Climate change 2021: The physical science basis* (Working Group I contribution to the Sixth Assessment Report). Retrieved from <https://www.ipcc.ch/>

Intergovernmental Panel on Climate Change. (2022). *Climate change 2022: Mitigation of climate change* (Working Group III contribution to the Sixth Assessment Report). Retrieved from <https://www.ipcc.ch/>

Intergovernmental Panel on Climate Change. (2023). *Climate change 2023 – Synthesis Report: A report of the Intergovernmental Panel on Climate Change.* Retrieved from <https://www.ipcc.ch/>

International Monetary Fund. (2023). *Climate Crossroads: Fiscal policies in a warming world.* Retrieved from <https://www.imf.org/en/Publications/FM/Issues/2023/10/10/fiscal-monitor-october-2023>

International Review of the Red Cross. (2017). Migration and displacement, 99(1), 153–178. <https://doi.org/10.1017/S1816383118000255>

Jänicke, M. (2008). Ecological modernization: New perspectives. *Journal of Cleaner Production, 13,* 557–565.

Jefferson, C. J., & Heathcott, J. (2003). *Beyond the ruins: The meanings of deindustrialization.* Cornell University Press.

Jessop, B. (2003). Changes in welfare regimes and the search for flexibility and employability. In H. Overbeek (Ed.), *The political economy of European unemployment: European integration and the transnationalization of the employment question* (pp. 29–50). Routledge.

Judt, T. (2010). *Ill fares the land.* Penguin Books.

Kalmar, I. (2022). *White but not quite: Central Europe's illiberal revolt.* University of Bristol Press.

Keller, J. (2010). *Tři sociální světy: Sociální struktura postindustriální společnosti.* Sociologické nakladatelství (SLON).

Kilbourne, W. E., & Carlson, L. (2008). The dominant social paradigm, consumption, and environmental attitudes: Can micromarketing education help? *Journal of Macromarketing, 28,* 106–121.

Klein, A., Schulze, M., & Vonyó, T. (2017). *How Peripheral was the Periphery? Industrialization in East Central Europe since 1870.* In K. H. O'Rourke & J. G. Williamson (Eds.), *The Spread of Modern Industry to the Periphery since 1871* (pp. 63–91). Oxford: Oxford University Press.

Komárek, V., et al. (1990). *Prognóza a program.* Academia. ISBN 8020002553.

Lefale, P. F. (2008). Beyond science: Climate change as a perfect political dilemma. *Political Science, 60*(1), 9–18.

Martinec, P., & Schejbalová, B. (2004). History and environmental impact of mining in the Ostrava–Karviná coal field (Upper Silesian coal basin, Czech Republic). *Geologica Belgica, 7*(3–4), 215–223.

Marx, K. (2020) [1863]. *Theories of surplus value: Volume I* (Radical Reprint).

Marx, K. (2023) [1857]. *Grundrisse: Foundations of a critique of political economy* (Grapevine edition).

McCormick, J. (2001). *Environmental policy in the European Union.* Palgrave.

Meadowcroft, J. (2005). From welfare state to eco-state. In J. Barry & R. Eckersley (Eds.), *The state and the global ecological crisis and the nation-state* (pp. 11–27). MIT Press.

Meadows, D. L., Meadows, D., Randers, J., & Behrensom, W. (1972). *The limits to growth: A report for the Club of Rome's Project on the Predicament of Mankind.* Earthscan.

Meadows, D., Randers, J., & Meadows, D. L. (2004). *Limits to growth: The 30-year update.* Green Publishing Company.

Mearsheimer, J. (2014). *The tragedy of great power politics* (Updated ed.). W. W. Norton & Company.

Milanović, B. (2019). *Capitalism, alone: The future of the system that rules the world.* Harvard University Press.

Milbrath, L. (1984). *Environmentalists: Vanguards for a new society.* State University of New York Press.

Millennium Ecosystem Assessment. (2005). *Ecosystems and human well-being: Current state and trends: Findings of the Condition and Trends Working Group.* Island Press.

Mohamed, M. D. S. (1990). Keynote address by the Honourable Dato' Seri Dr Mahathir Mohamed, the Prime Minister of Malaysia. (1990 statement during a meeting of European and Asian leaders).

Mol, A. (2000). The environmental movement in an era of ecological modernization. *Geoforum, 31,* 45–56.

Network of Central Banks and Supervisors for Greening the Financial System. (2023). *NGFS climate scenarios for central banks and supervisors: Long-term scenarios (Phase IV).* Retrieved from <https://www.ngfs.net/

sites/default/files/medias/documents/ngfs_climate_scenarios_for_central_banks_and_supervisors_phase_iv.pdf>

O'Connor, J. (1988). Capitalism, nature, socialism: A theoretical introduction. *Capitalism Nature Socialism, 1*, 11–39.

O'Connor, J. (1994). Is sustainable capitalism possible? In M. O'Connor (Ed.), *Is capitalism sustainable?* (pp. 20–39). Guilford Press.

Paterson, M. (2007). Environmental politics: Sustainability and the politics of transformation. *International Political Science Review, 28*, 545–556.

Pickvance, C. G. (1999). Democratisation and the decline of social movements: The effects of regime change on collective action in Eastern Europe, Southern Europe, and Latin America. *Sociology, 33*(2), 353–372.

Pisani-Ferry, J., & Tagliapietra, S. (2024). An investment strategy to keep the European Green Deal on track. *Policy Brief, 31/24*. (December 2024).

Polanyi, K. (1944). *The great transformation*. Rinehart and Company.

Ponting, C. (2007). *A new green history of the world: The environment and the collapse of great civilizations*. Vintage Books.

Raudsepp-Hearne, C., Peterson, G. D., Tengö, M., Bennett, E. M., Holland, T., Benessaiah, K., McDonald, G. K., & Pfeifer, L. (2010). Untangling the environmentalist's paradox: Why is human well-being increasing as ecosystem services degrade? *BioScience, 60*(8), 576–589.

Rostow, W. W. (1960). *The stages of economic growth: A non-Communist manifesto*. University Press.

Sadler Committee Report. (1832). *Report of the Select Committee on Factory Children's Labour (Parliamentary Papers 1831–32, Volume XV)*. Retrieved from <https://history.hanover.edu/courses/excerpts/111sad.html>

Sarre, P., & Jehlička, P. (2007). Environmental movements in space-time: The Czech and Slovak republics from Stalinism to post-socialism. *Transactions of the Institute of British Geographers, 32*(3), 346–362.

Schiller, H. I. (1996). *Information inequality: The deepening social crisis in America*. Routledge.

Schmidheiny, S. (2002). The sustainable development business: Enterprises and countries in global competition [Paper presented at the Ethos Conference, Sao Paulo, Brazil]. Retrieved 5 June 2010, from <http://www.stephanschmidheiny.net/speeches-and-conferences/>

Schnaiberg, A. (1980). *The environment: From surplus to scarcity.* Oxford University Press.

Schnaiberg, A. (2009). Labor productivity and the environment. In K. A. Gould & T. L. Lewis (Eds.), *Twenty lessons in environmental sociology.* Oxford University Press.

Schumacher, E. F. (1973). *Small is beautiful: A study of economics as if people mattered.* Hartley & Marks Publishers.

Schumpeter, J. (2021). *The theory of economic development.* Routledge.

Sennett, R. (2006). *The culture of the new capitalism.* Yale University Press.

Skjaerseth, J. B., & Wettestad, J. (2007). Is EU enlargement bad for environmental policy? Confronting gloomy expectations with evidence. *International Environmental Agreements, 7,* 263–280.

Sklair, L. (2000). *The transnational capitalist class and the discourse of globalization.* (Unpublished paper, Department of Sociology, London School of Economics and Political Science).

Smith, M. (2001). Face of nature: Environmental ethics and the boundaries of contemporary social theory. *Current Sociology, 49,* 49–65.

Spaargaren, G., & Mol, A. (1992). Sociology, environment, and modernity: Ecological modernization as a theory of social change. *Society and Natural Resources, 55,* 323–344.

Steingart, G. (2008). *The war for wealth: The true story of globalization, or why the flat world is broken: The truth about globalization, and why the flat world is broken.* McGraw-Hill Education Ltd.

Stern, H. (2006). *The economics of climate change: The Stern Review.* Cambridge University Press.

Stivers, R. (1976). *The sustainable society: Ethics and economic growth.* Westminster Press.

The Economics of Ecosystems and Biodiversity (TEEB). (2008). *The economics of ecosystems and biodiversity: An interim report.* TEEB Project. Retrieved 5 September 2010, from <http://www.teebweb.org/LinkClick.aspx?fileticket=I4Y2nqqIiCg%3D&tabid=1278&language=en-US>

The Economics of Ecosystems and Biodiversity (TEEB). (2009). *The economics of ecosystems and biodiversity: Climate issues update.* TEEB Project. Retrieved 5 September 2010, from <http://www.teebweb.org/

LinkClick.aspx?fileticket=L6XLPaoaZv8%3D&tabid=1278&language=en-US>

Tietenberg, T. (1992). *Environmental and natural resource economics.* HarperCollins Publishers.

Turner, G. (2008). *A comparison of 'The Limits to Growth' with thirty years of reality.* CSIRO.

Turnovec, F. (1998). *Czech Republic '97: The Year of Crisis.* Prague: CERGE/EI.

Tusk, D. (2025). The speech of Polish Prime Minister at the European Parliament: 'Europe is not yet lost as long as we are alive.' (Delivered 22 January 2025). Retrieved from <https://polish-presidency.consilium. europa.eu/en/news/the-speech-of-polish-prime-minister-at-the-european-parliament-europe-is-not-yet-lost-as-long-as-we-are-alive/>

United Nations High Commissioner for Refugees. (2015). *Over one million sea arrivals reach Europe in 2015.* Retrieved from <https:// www.unhcr.org/news/stories/over-one-million-sea-arrivals-reach-europe-2015#:~:text=UNHCR's%20latest%20figures%20show%20 that,3%2C735%20were%20missing%2C%20believed%20drowned>

Veblen, T. (1899). *The theory of the leisure class.* Prometheus Books.

Wallerstein, I. (2000). *The essential Wallerstein.* The New York Press.

Wallerstein, I. (2002). A movement of movement? New revolts against the system. *New Left Review, 18,* 29–39.

Wallerstein, I. (2004). *World-system analysis.* Duke University Press.

Wallerstein, I. (2005). After developmentalism and globalization: What? *Social Forces, 83,* 321–336.

Wei, Q. (2021). Explaining the emergence of low-carbon forerunner cities based on the interaction effects of different governance processes: A case study of China's low-carbon pilot. *Carbon Management, 12*(1), 81–92. <https://doi.org/10.1080/17583004.2021.1876530>

William, M., & Lafferty, W. M. (1998). *Democracy and ecological rationality: New trials for an old ceremony.* Paper presented at the CPSA/IPSA Roundtable – Integration and Disintegration: New Partnerships in the World Order, Quebec, Canada, 12–13 February 1998. Retrieved 5 June 2010, from <http://www.prosus.uio.no/publikasjoner/Andre_pub/1. html>

World Commission on Environment and Development. (1987). *Our common future*. Oxford University Press.

World Economic Forum. (2023). *Climate change is costing the world $16 million per hour: Study*. Retrieved from <https://www.weforum. org/stories/2023/10/climate-loss-and-damage-cost-16-million-per-hour/#:~:text=Writer%2C%20EcoWatch-,The%20global%20cost%20 of%20climate%20change%20damage%20is%20estimated%20 to,%2C%20agriculture%2C%20and%20human%20health>

Index